Studies in British Industry No. 2
General Editor: Sylvia Trench, M.A. (Oxon.)
Lecturer in Industrial Economics in the University of Nottingham

Nationalisation in
British Industry

Nationalisation in British Industry

by L. J. Tivey

Lecturer in Public Administration at
the University of Birmingham

Jonathan Cape
Thirty Bedford Square
London

First Published 1966
© 1966 by L. J. Tivey

Printed and bound in Great Britain
by Cox & Wyman Ltd,
London, Fakenham and Reading

Contents

Preface

The nature and scope of this book are explained in Chapter 1. It is intended to serve as an introduction to the study of nationalisation, and no more; all the problems that it raises can be more fully pursued elsewhere. But for the student and general reader there may be some virtue in brevity: from a short book the interrelations of various topics may emerge more clearly, and so it may be easier to see the subject as a whole. It should be stressed, however, that no attempt has been made to discuss the problems of the power industries, or of transport, as such; for this purpose the reader should turn to studies in industrial economics.

I would like to thank friends who have commented on various parts of the book, including Messrs E. L. Pritchard, A. L. Minkes, D. Rimmer, J. M. Samuels, S. C. Littlechild, G. F. McRobie, Dr N. S. Ross, and Mrs S. Trench. Their advice has always been stimulating and helpful, and often acceptable. The faults that remain are my own.

Faculty of Commerce and Social Science,   L. J. TIVEY
University of Birmingham
February 1966

The Scope of
Nationalisation

This is a book on a political subject. Politics are concerned essentially with divergence and disagreement, and this is therefore an account of controversies and the outcome of controversies. Politics are also concerned with the way disagreements are resolved, and hence the book also discusses the arrangements for the administration of institutions and the settlement of policies. Finally, since politics are often about a conflict between ends rather than means, the purposes which the institutions try to serve are discussed.

The institutions to be considered are the British nationalised industries. The political fact of their nationalised status is the main focus of interest for this book. It is this status that the industries have in common, and it is this that makes them worth discussing together.

They are, nevertheless, industrial organisations. They buy, produce, and sell as economic units, and it is impossible to conceive them apart from their economic nature. Much of the material must be presented, therefore, in economic terms. My object is not to solve, or even to express views on, the economic problems as such, but to consider them as part of the policy-making process. For economists, my aim is to show how the nature of institutions shapes the issues with which they grapple—to show the extent to which these issues can be attributed to, or are affected by, the nationalised status of the industries. It is deceptively easy for economists to examine industrial problems as if they were in a vacuum; but in fact, the control, organisation, and purposes of nationalisation are central facts that cannot be realistically ignored.

The general plan of the book may be briefly indicated. The next chapter describes the development of ideas about nationalisation, both in the sense of public ownership and of its embodiment in the public corporation. The third chapter describes the circumstances in which nationalisation first took place, the parliamentary process of legislation, and the basic structure of public corporations as they have emerged. The fourth chapter sets out briefly something about nationalisation in practice and the industrial record of the corporations. These three chapters are largely historical and factual, though for the sake of brevity some general judgments have been used to summarise complex situations.

The rest of the book is concerned with the examination of problems and controversies. In Chapter 5 these are problems of internal organisation; in Chapter 6 they are problems of external relations: with the Government, with Parliament, and with the public. Chapters 7 and 8 consider fundamental issues. In one the objectives to be aimed at in industries already nationalised are considered; in the other there is a return to the theme of Chapter 2, the case for nationalisation and public ownership as such. In these later chapters the intention has been to set out the problems and arguments fairly, but this has not prevented assessments being made and conclusions drawn on many matters.

The scope of the book is conveniently limited by institutional boundaries: it covers the public corporations running nationalised industries in coal, electricity, gas, inland transport, and air transport. It should scarcely be necessary to stress the economic importance of these bodies. The accompanying table sets out the public corporations, as the pattern had evolved by 1963, and shows their output and the numbers employed by them. These figures give some idea of the relative importance of the various bodies and of their place in the country's economic system. It will be seen that there are two very large (coal and the railways), two large (electricity and gas), and a number of lesser industries. The situation in other countries is described at the end of Chapter 3.

It is now common practice to describe Britain's economy as 'mixed'; that is, it is partly private enterprise and partly in public ownership. Associated with this notion are the concepts of 'public sector' and 'private sector' of the economy.

	Total revenue (£ million)	Number of Employees (thousands)	Percentage of working population
National Coal Board	1,147*	517·0	2·1
Electricity Council and Boards	912	210·4	0·8
North Scotland Hydro-Electric Board	21	3·5	–
South Scotland Electricity Board	81	16·0	–
Gas Council and Boards	479	123·1	0·5
British Railways Board	460	464·3	1·8
London Transport Board	100·5	74·0	0·3
British Transport Docks Board	23·0	13·7	–
British Waterways Board	4·5	3·8	–
Transport Holding Company	17·5†	100·0	0·4
British Overseas Airways Corporation	104·8	21·1	–
British European Airways	59·8	17·1	–
Total, nationalised industries	3,418·1	1,564·0	8·2
Total, public sector		5,812·0	23·2
TOTAL		25,071·0‡	100·0

* Fifteen months, 1963–4
† Profit, not revenue
‡ Working population, Great Britain

These terms must be used, if at all, with very great care. They originate in the national income accounting used for evaluating and guiding general economic policy, and their application in political and administrative discussion can be highly misleading. In the present context it should be remembered that the 'public sector' includes many institutions besides nationalised industries, most of them bearing very little similarity to the public corporations discussed in this book. In particular it includes Government departments and local authorities, both of which operate public and social services of considerable economic weight. The structure and purposes of the other parts of the 'public sector' are often very different from those of industrial organisations, and the idea of a 'public sector' as an harmonious administrative unity is a myth.

The private sector includes both private-enterprise firms and individual people. All business activity takes place in a civil order shaped over time by governments, and its success depends in part on the success of the Government's economic policies. In addition, the Government actively promotes for private industry, in one way or another, research, productivity, marketing, training and technical education, and exports; it operates a protective tariff and in special cases provides finance. In short, the expression 'mixed economy' implies not only that some industry is privately owned and some publicly, but also that the economic efforts of government, firms, and individuals are closely interwoven and do not operate independently.

The public sector is generally reckoned to comprise about twenty-five per cent of the economy, measured in terms of production, and to employ about a quarter of the country's working population. The nationalised industries themselves produce about ten per cent of Britain's wealth annually, and they employ about eight per cent of the labour force. Their position as basic industries or services, however, makes them crucial to the rest of the economy.

The Origins of
Nationalisation

'Nationalisation, then, is not an end, but a means to an end,' wrote R. H. Tawney in 1921, 'and when the question of ownership has been settled the question of administration remains for solution.'[1]

Both questions are discussed in this book; and in seeking the sources of nationalisation in Britain, we shall find it convenient to distinguish two developments, approximating to these questions. The first was political — there was in the first half of the twentieth century a growing belief in the need for a measure of public ownership of productive forces. The second was administrative — there was in the same period a great increase in the number of institutions of a 'semi-independent' type, neither part of the ordinary governmental structure nor yet totally separate from it. The conjunction of these developments in the programme of the Labour Party in mid-century brought about the main nationalised industries in their present form.

In this chapter the two developments will be examined in turn.

BELIEF IN PUBLIC OWNERSHIP

It is prudent to be clear about 'ownership' itself before considering its private and public forms. The concept of ownership is not a simple one. It implies a relationship in which men exercise certain rights over goods, or 'property'. The rights must be recognised by law, for ownership is inherently a legal concept.

Among the rights usually involved are the right to dispose of the goods — by gift, by sale or exchange, by bequest; the right to use and the right to deny use to others; and the right to enjoy the fruits of the property. These rights are not immutable — they may be varied by differences in the law, by different systems of tenure, or by social custom. Nevertheless, with the growth of modern industry, the existence of this group of rights ensured that the owners of industrial property—urban land, factories, mines—became the employers of labour and the managers of the various enterprises. This is capitalism—a system in which ultimate control lies with the persons who have a legal title to the capital.

Not all property belongs to individuals. Groups of people can enjoy ownership rights collectively, and in practice most modern industry is now in the hands of business firms—companies or corporations. Moreover, there is the distinction between private and public ownership. Some property is owned by the community as a whole and controlled by the Government of the nation. This book deals with those *industries* that are owned in this way in Britain, and not with other Government property.

Modern ideas of public ownership began to take shape in the nineteenth century. Many socialist ideas, including that of common ownership, have a much longer history. Indeed, in Plato's *Republic* the ruling classes hold all their possessions in common. There was a tradition of socialist ideas in Europe in the Middle Ages, and in Sir Thomas More's *Utopia* of 1516 the ideal society takes the form of a co-operative commonwealth.

But these and other antecedents are of doubtful relevance. The industrial revolution brought with it a revolution in thinking about society, and the ideas that are most significant for twentieth-century nationalisation arose as criticisms of the new industrial civilisation. (The word 'socialism' first appeared in 1827 in a magazine of the co-operative movement.) Socialism is now generally taken to be a rival system to capitalism for the organisation of economic affairs. Politically it has meant more than the substitution of common ownership for private ownership. It has been associated with the general emancipation of the working class, and it has emphasised the need for greater equality in economic and social matters. The socialist movement has always been divided, moreover, into many schools of thought; some, like Marxism, claiming to be scientific, and others stressing Christian or other moral values. But all socialists

have insisted on the evils of capitalist ownership and have endea-
voured to find better arrangements. The crucial point about modern
socialism, as distinct from earlier schemes for common ownership
and communal living, is that it concentrates its attention on 'the
means of production', not personal possessions. Industry in the
nineteenth century became an affair of large organisations, and it is
the public ownership of industrial enterprises of this type that nine-
teenth- and twentieth-century socialists have advocated.

This is no place to relate the wider history of socialism in Britain.[2]
After the death of Robert Owen and the decay of his ideas for co-
operation and model communities, socialism achieved little prominence in mid-Victorian England. It was on the international scene
that Marx and Engels were giving a new profundity to socialist
ideas. Common ownership of the means of production was a cardinal aim of the Marxist programme, and it thus became a leading
element in left-wing thought everywhere. But Marxism never
secured the dominance in England that it did in Europe. The Fabian
Society and other groups advocated non-capitalist ownership on
practical and moral grounds, and preferred a pragmatic political
strategy. The eventual accomplishment of some public ownership
in Britain cannot be understood merely as the rise and triumph of
a single doctrine. Not merely were its socialist advocates a varied
and often dissonant army, but its progress was aided by many non-
socialist forces. Thus it is possible for some socialists to be critical
of common ownership in the forms it has taken, and where it does
not reflect the other values that they seek to promote.

The economic trends which led to public ownership were two-
fold. On the one hand there was technological development which
bred industrial change; and many of the new industries and services
needed to be organised as monopolies for full efficiency. On the
other hand depression brought special difficulties to particular
industries. It was argued that these needed reconstruction by
national ownership.

Many of the arguments for public ownership, however, were not
economic in character at all. In the nineteenth century, protests
against the evils of industrialism were also protests against capitalism.

John Ruskin and William Morris were critics of the moral and artistic
state of civilisation—they found industrial Britain ugly and philis-
tine. When Ruskin entitled an essay 'A Joy for Ever, and its Price in
the Market', he was satirising the application of economic criteria to
the deeper satisfactions of human life, and his criticism of uncon-
trolled free enterprise was that it overvalued economic success, not
that it failed to achieve it. Again, the criticism of R. H. Tawney in
the twentieth century was moral and religious: a capitalist society
was an acquisitive society—one in which material gain was honoured
before service and co-operation. Finally there were criticisms from a
specifically political standpoint. H. J. Laski, for example, argued
that the wealth accruing to private industrialists gave them unfair
political advantages, and that neither individual liberties nor democratic procedures would be respected by capitalist owners of industry
if their position were attacked.

The defence of capitalism depended largely on the theory of free
competition, as developed by economists. This varied in dogmatism
and in sophistication, but fundamentally it always asserted that
economic welfare was best promoted by individuals seeking their
own betterment, for in society they could only do this by providing
goods and services for their fellows. Given competition, privately
owned firms would have both the motives and the pressures to make
themselves efficient. Politically and morally, capitalism was seen as
essentially liberal—it did not impose restrictions on individual
efforts, it rewarded talent and enterprise, and it limited the power
and influence of the Government. In the long run, it was claimed,
all human freedoms were involved in freedom of economic activity,
for on this freedom rested the ability of men to live independently
of the control of Government.

Five factors

It is possible to distinguish five main factors which led to the
mid-twentieth-century political situation which shaped industrial
nationalisation in Britain. The first four are described in a very rough
chronological order of origin—thus the co-operative movement
began in the mid-nineteenth century, the Labour Party started in

1900, the movement for workers' control flourished around the First World War, and the need for planning emerged between the wars. Finally, there were non-socialist influences at work. But the influence of all still persists.

(1) *The rise and limitations of consumers' co-operation.* If business undertakings are not controlled by the owners of the capital, other groups may take charge. In the British retail co-operative movement, which began with the Rochdale pioneers in 1844, control is ultimately in the hands of the consumer-members. Though these consumers may have small capital holdings, their rights over the management of the societies derive entirely from the fact of membership. Any person may join, and each member is entitled to one vote, which cannot be multiplied either by investment or purchases. The retail societies, controlled by consumers, control in turn bodies like the Co-operative Wholesale Society which engage in manufacturing and distributing. The workers in all parts of the movement are employees, subordinate to the management in the usual way.

This movement, which had sales of £50 million a year by 1900 and over £1,000 million in the 1960s, was the first clear large-scale breakaway from capitalist organisation. Its success must be considered a convincing demonstration of the viability of other such forms of enterprise. But with the twentieth century the limitations of this approach became apparent. It was based on retailing: consumer control over manufacturing was remote and confined to lines to be traded in the shops. The system could make no impact on the basic industries or on the risky expanding manufacturing businesses. Many great industries sell little to the individual consumer but trade mainly with other firms. Reformers have never ceased to hope for further application of the consumer co-operative principle, but in the twentieth century it has never seemed likely to suit the problem industries. It has offered little to advocates of workers' control, and, more significantly in the event, it has not provided convincingly the guarantees of dynamic management that were thought necessary.

(2) *The Labour Party and its programme.* In 1900 a group of trade unions and socialist societies came together to found the Labour Party, which aimed at securing distinctive representation of the

workers in Parliament. In itself this implied the desirability of democratic political action and the imposition on industry of change by legislation. At first there was no agreed doctrine of what those changes were to be. Many leading trade unionists supported the Liberal Party and were openly non-socialist. Others regarded socialists without hostility, but as rather impractical idealists. Resolutions favourable to nationalisation were first passed by the Trades Union Congress in the 1880s and 1890s. In 1894 a motion for the nationalisation 'of the means of production, distribution and exchange' was successful, but in 1895 this demand was modified to mean nationalisation only of land, minerals, and railways. At the time of the foundation of the Labour Party, the trade union element could not be regarded as committed to widespread nationalisation. Nevertheless many unions were in a radical mood, dissatisfied with the results of working with the Liberals, and very conscious that political action was necessary to protect the position of the unions and to help the workers generally. In the period before the First World War, various nationalisation motions were carried by the T.U.C. and some nationalisation Bills introduced in the House of Commons, for purposes of demonstration, by the minority of Labour Members of Parliament; but these actions were overshadowed, in the Labour movement as well as outside it, by more urgent industrial and political issues.

The real beginning of the Labour Party's concern with public ownership came at the end of the First World War, and it roughly coincided with the Party's replacement of the Liberals as the main rival to the Conservatives. The experiences of war had forced trade unionists, like others, into a more radical frame of mind; and they had been impressed by the effectiveness of Government control of industry during the war, which seemed to show that business competition was not necessarily the most efficient method of conducting affairs. Trades Union Congresses during the war demanded increasingly wider measures of nationalisation.

The Labour Party was put on a new footing in 1918, with a new constitution. Clause Four of this document stated the objective of the Party:

To secure for the producers by hand or brain the full fruits of their industry, and the most equitable distribution thereof that may be possible, upon the basis of the common ownership of the means of production, and the best obtainable system of popular administration and control of each industry and service.

The Labour Party's election programme in December 1918 was called *Labour and the New Social Order*, and included wide proposals for social and fiscal reform. Moreover, it contained specific and far-ranging proposals for public ownership: land was to be taken into common ownership gradually; coal, railways, and electricity were to be nationalised; industrial and life insurance were to be taken over; municipalities were to control the drink trade and were encouraged to take up new enterprises such as the retailing of coal and milk. Monopoly industries were also to be nationalised when convenient.

Henceforward the Labour Party was clearly a socialist party aiming at large measures of public ownership in industry. The growing strength of the Party and the militancy of the large trade unions—who were by this time also demanding nationalisation—meant that public ownership became for the first time the key issue in British domestic politics—a position it retained for forty years.

The Labour Party made chequered progress between the wars, forming Governments in 1924 and 1929 but never securing a large majority in the House of Commons. It was never, therefore, in a position to implement the nationalisation plans which it put forward repeatedly at elections. In the 1930s there was much dissension between the left wing, led by Sir Stafford Cripps, and the rest of the Party. But ideas about priorities for nationalisation crystallised, and a workable programme was indicated in Dr Hugh Dalton's book, *Practical Socialism for Britain*, in 1935. This advocated among other things the public ownership of transport, coalmining, power, steel, armaments, and gradually of the land.

The depression and industrial strife of the inter-war years, of course, confirmed socialists in their dissatisfaction with capitalist

ownership, and reinforced their determination to carry through
drastic changes. By the outbreak of the Second World War, the
Labour Party had its industrial outlook and priorities clear.

(3) *Workers' control.* Before the Labour Party could be sure of the
type of socialism it wished to promote, however, it had to consider
the currents of opinion among its likely supporters. Capitalism was
a system under which labour was hired by capital-owners—and it
was natural, since this was the system under criticism, that a simple
reversal of control should be considered.

The most elaborate doctrines of workers' control were developed
on the Continent, where they were known as syndicalism. In
Britain the principle took the modified form of guild socialism.
As advocated by A. R. Orage (in a magazine called *The New Age*),
and by A. J. Penty, S. G. Hobson, and G. D. H. Cole in various books
and pamphlets, this envisaged a system whereby each industry was
owned and controlled by a workers' guild. Direction would have
been in the hands of elected workers' representatives and of Government nominees charged with the duty of protecting the consumers.

Two themes animated the proposals of guild socialists. The first
was the need to liberate workers in their daily routine in the
factories. Changes, such as Government ownership, which made no
immediate change in the relations between employer and employee,
were condemned as inadequate. A transformation in the direct
control of the workers' lives was needed. Secondly, the guild
socialists were strong advocates of the representation of interests
and were distrustful of assemblies (like the House of Commons)
based on geographical constituencies. An employer, in their view,
whether he was elected or not, could not possibly represent a working man. They therefore proposed schemes for national assemblies
elected by occupational constituencies.

Guild socialism as such faded quickly after the end of the First
World War. Its institutional proposals were at once crude and
idealistic. They had little appeal to the militant yet hard-headed
and experienced socialist leaders of the time, who saw in the existing
political machinery opportunities for achieving effective power.
Among the intellectuals the preference of Fabians like the Webbs for

Government or municipal ownership was not to be overcome. But among trade unionists there persisted—certainly until the 1930s and to some extent beyond—a demand for workers' *participation*, at least. Some share in control, that is to say, was desired; and this feeling was not easily denied. In the end only minimum concessions to this point of view were made; what they were will emerge later in the chapter.

(4) *The need for national economic planning.* The idea of economic planning by central authorities is a comparatively new one. It was not much discussed by Marxists or by Fabians before the First World War. When the Communists came to power in Russia, however, they were faced with the problem of running a collectivised economy, and it was by a series of five-year plans that they imposed order and direction on economic activity. The notion of a centrally directed economy came under strong attack by anti-socialist economists between the wars.[3] It was argued very strongly that without a free market from which freely negotiated prices could emerge, the controllers of enterprises (publicly or privately owned) would have no guide by which to make rational production decisions. Nor would a central directorate have any means of relating their programmes to what people actually wanted.

The socialist response to these criticisms varied. But those whose views were influential in the British Labour Party accepted the necessity of free consumer demand and tried to devise methods by which publicly owned enterprises (i.e. those without the desire for profit) would respond to it. To do this a considerable degree of autonomy had to be granted to public enterprises, and—as described later in this chapter—this requirement favoured the public corporation as the vehicle of nationalisation.

In the same period between the wars, however, some industrialists and some economists were beginning to doubt whether free competition was sufficient by itself to ensure economic welfare. The National Government abandoned free trade in 1933, and numerous schemes of regulation were promoted by Government and businessmen alike. The decisive change for non-socialists came, however, with the publication and acceptance of J. M. Keynes's *General*

Theory of Employment, Interest and Money in the years before 1939. This provided what had been lacking, to some extent in socialist as well as non-socialist ideas: an economic rationale for general Government control, as distinct from piecemeal intervention.

Socialists believed that Keynesian planning reinforced their case for public ownership in industry. Only if major industries were owned and directly controlled, they argued, could investment be stimulated and the public sector exert a steadying influence on the economy. The inter-war depression, and the belief that central planning might relieve it, helped to reconcile many people to the idea of a controlled economy. And, in the 1930s especially, there was a strong feeling on the left that private enterprise would not co-operate with a Labour Government. The degree of control needed for planning would therefore necessitate nationalisation — perhaps on a greater scale than that originally envisaged.

Many believers in central economic planning, of course, were not socialists and did not accept the need for widespread public ownership. Indeed, the acceptance of Keynesian economic ideas did not seem to everyone to involve planning as such, and the post-war years in Britain saw much controversy about the best type of full-employment measures to adopt. But by this time the Labour Government had established the basic nationalised industries.

(5) *Non-socialist influences.* At all times there have been people who would not accept any general socialist doctrines but were nevertheless prepared to advocate nationalisation of particular industries or services. Joseph Chamberlain promoted a great deal of municipal enterprise in Birmingham. Mr Gladstone nationalised telegraphs in 1869 and at one time contemplated railway nationalisation. Mr Winston Churchill declared in 1918, 'The Government policy is the nationalisation of the railways. That great step it has at last been decided to take.'[4] In fact, that Government contented itself with amalgamation. But between the wars there was a slow spread of ad hoc public ownership — the B.B.C., London Transport, the electricity grid, and coal royalties are examples. There were also reports between 1936 and 1945 on certain industries — MacGowan on electricity, Heyworth on gas, and Reid on coal — which recom-

mended action so drastic that many thought it would not come about without nationalisation.

Perhaps the argument that appealed most strongly to non-socialists was the monopoly one. In cases where monopoly was natural or desirable, then public ownership might provide necessary safeguards. This was not incompatible with belief in a generally competitive system or in the greater drive and initiative of private enterprise.

The development of these sorts of opinions, together with the isolated acts of public ownership by non-socialist governments, seemed to many observers to confirm the existence of an irreversible trend. There was much talk of inevitable Government control and ownership 'whatever party is in power'. Marxists of course believed in general historical laws, by which broad future developments could be predicted. But those who rejected this outlook found the pressure of twentieth-century developments impressive, and the belief that increased collectivism was in some sense an unavoidable trend of the times was very fashionable until about 1950. The Conservative Governments of the 1950s managed to check the spread of collectivism; but it was no more than a check, not a reversal, and there are signs of further extensions of Government activity in the 1960s.

It is easy to regard the growth of public control and planning entirely in intellectual terms—as a change in both academic and popular ideas about the economic role of Government. There is of course a good deal of truth in this. There has been a considerable movement of opinion. But the change was not merely a matter of people revising their views: there has been a transformation in the nature of the economy and of society. It is not a case of new ideas being applied to old situations and unchanged industries. Rather, the development of the structure and industrial content of society has led partly to a revision of doctrine, and partly to different results from the application of old criteria.

Thus among the publicly organised activities of today there are many that scarcely existed at all at the turn of the century. Some of them, such as electricity and air transport, began as private enterprises under public regulation. Radio and television have been, in Britain, predominantly public enterprises. Atomic energy has always been a Government concern. The internal-combustion engine has led to great public concern with roads and road haulage. Some existing Government activities, such as telecommunications, have enhanced importance through technological development.

During the period between the two world wars, the forces that shaped British nationalisation were built up. The experience of the inter-war period was in the minds of the Labour Party politicians who carried out the main nationalisation measures after the Second World War. So far, however, this chapter has dealt with the growth of the *desire* to nationalise. To some extent the rejection of consumers' or workers' control decided the character of non-capitalist enterprise: the only other possibility was ownership by the community as a whole, through the machinery of government. But the form taken by common ownership — the institutions necessary for its embodiment — were matters of vital importance. It is to the evolution of the public corporation, therefore, that attention must now be given.

RISE OF THE PUBLIC CORPORATION

In the nineteenth century the foundations of the modern British administrative system were laid. The dominant reforms of the period were liberal and utilitarian in spirit. They aimed at efficiency, honesty, and impartiality. It was not envisaged that many trading activities would be carried on by the Government; fairness and economy would be the guiding principles of those that were.

Government departments were in origin the offices of ministers, and until the middle of the nineteenth century they were staffed in a haphazard way. In 1854 a report by Sir Stafford Northcote and Sir Charles Trevelyan set out a scheme for a new unified Civil Service. It was to be a permanent career service, working loyally and impartially for changing political masters, and was to be divided between clerical and superior positions. These principles were gradually put into effect, and by the end of the century they dominated the administrative structure of the central Government. Departments

are under the direct control of ministers, who are responsible for
all that their departments do—they must answer in Parliament for
minor details of administration as well as major policy.[5] Civil servants
influence policy by advising ministers: they have no authority of
their own, and act always in the name of the Minister. In dealings
with the public their discretion is usually limited, and in their
striving for impartiality there is, traditionally, fairly close conformity
to rules and precedents. Money is provided annually by Parliament
and must be spent on the purpose for which it was authorised.

The main trading organisation of the Government in the nineteenth century was the Post Office. This is a Government department
like the others, staffed by civil servants and controlled by a responsible Minister, the Postmaster-General. Until 1933 it was operated
virtually like any other department. Since then there has been an
increasing adaptation to commercial practice.

There was one other nineteenth-century administrative body of
importance: the local authority. This consists of an elected council
controlling a variety of departments, many of which have large
staffs. Thus local services, including trading services, are under the
direct supervision of elected politicians. At one time the extension
of municipal trading was regarded as a main route for public
enterprise,[6] but in the twentieth century the urgent problems of
coalmining, railways, and electricity demanded national solutions.
Municipalisation has therefore been overshadowed by nationalisation.

The principle that all public administrative bodies should be
directly subordinate to elected authorities was firmly maintained
between 1855 and 1905.[7] In this period the experience of the Poor
Law Commission set up in 1834 was held to be decisive. Widespread criticism of the Commission had had little effect on its
administration, and no minister had been able to control its actions
or, when necessary, to defend them. The Commissioners were
stigmatised as The Three Kings of Somerset House, and after the
replacement of the Commission in 1847, the idea of independence or
autonomy in administration was under a cloud for the rest of the
century.

The growth of Government activity in this century has involved the abandonment of this principle. There were one or two examples of new non-departmental authorities before 1914; after the First World War, however, the number of such bodies grew steadily. The changes were not unforeseen, or unopposed. In 1918 a Government committee under Lord Haldane declared:

> We are so far from thinking that the importance of a service to the community is *prima facie* a reason for making those who administer it immune from ordinary parliamentary criticism, that we feel all such proposals should be most carefully scrutinised, and that there should be no omission, in the case of any particular service, of those safeguards which Ministerial responsibility to Parliament alone provides.[8]

This opposition, however, had little effect.

It cannot be stressed too strongly that the growth of non-departmental administration has resulted in a great *variety* of institutions. Once the fixed principles of the Government department and full ministerial responsibility are abandoned, many degrees of control and many special relationships become possible. Some autonomous institutions, such as the British Council, are only a little different from departments. On the other hand there are bodies like the British Standards Institution, formally private and independent, which receive large, regular grants from the Government. Their purposes also vary greatly: some administer services, some regulate industries, some disburse funds, some are advisory, some quasi-judicial.

Nevertheless, among these twentieth-century autonomous institutions there can be no doubt that the public corporation is pre-eminent. Moreover, there lies behind the public corporation a theory and a fairly definite set of principles; the other autonomous bodies have developed in a much more confused and pragmatic way, with little background of deliberate principle.

The beginnings of the early public corporations — the forerunners of the present nationalised industries — can now be traced.

It is usual to begin with the Port of London Authority. At the beginning of the century the need for some reform was evident, and in 1902 a Royal Commission under Lord Revelstoke recommended placing the docks in the hands of a non-profit-making public trust. This was to be elected by port users, on the model of the Mersey Docks and Harbour Board of 1857. After attempts to legislate in 1903 and 1905 failed, the Port of London Act was finally passed in 1908. This provided for a Board with eighteen members elected by port users and ten appointed by public authorities, including Government departments and local authorities. The Authority owns and runs the docks and has powers of river conservancy. Representatives of labour serve on the board among the nominees of public authorities, but owners of Port of London stock have no share in control. In so far as the Authority was similar to other port trusts, its establishment could not be regarded as an unprecedented move. The Liberal Government of the period set up other non-departmental bodies, however, in the Road Board (1909) and the Insurance Commissions (1911), and though these were short-lived, it was clear that new (or revived) types of institutions were being sought for new Government activities.

In 1919 the Forestry Commission was established, modelled on the Ecclesiastical and Charity Commissions. Its duties are to maintain national forests and to carry out a programme of afforestation on waste land, for which powers of compulsory purchase are available. Its employees are civil servants; it is supported by Treasury grants since sales of timber cannot yet cover its costs; and since 1945 the Minister of Agriculture has had power to give general directions to it. Nevertheless it retains considerable operational independence from the Government machine. Also in 1919 a supervisory body for the electricity industry, the Electricity Commissioners, was set up. It had judicial and administrative duties, but power to reorganise the industry was struck out of the Bill by the House of Lords, which was to mean that structural changes in the industry were later necessary.

These developments were merely preliminary. The establishment of the public corporation in the form we now know it came in the late 'twenties, with the British Broadcasting Corporation and the

Central Electricity Board, followed by the London Passenger Transport Board in the early 'thirties.

Between 1922 and 1926 broadcasting in Britain was in the hands of the British Broadcasting Company Ltd, owned by radio-manufacturing companies. After the report of the Crawford Committee on broadcasting in 1925,[9] it was decided to replace this by a publicly owned but independently managed body, the British Broadcasting Corporation. It was clear by this stage that the new medium of communication had potentialities of great social and political consequence. Dislike of commercial radio as it was emerging in other countries, and the desire to establish a responsible and impartial source of public information, led many sections of opinion to favour a Governmental body. Nevertheless, close control by the Government of the day was unacceptable for political reasons, and it was doubted if an ordinary department would show adequate understanding of entertainment or cultural matters. The B.B.C. was thus essentially an attempt to insulate a public institution from partisan political interference; and it was designed —unlike most other public corporations—to avoid commercial operation. There was to be no advertising, and revenue was derived from the proportion of licence fees that the Government handed over to the B.B.C. A board of governors exercised general supervision, but real power lay with the Director-General. The first of these, Sir John Reith, was a man of determination and strict principle who imparted a good deal of his own austere character to the corporation. The Postmaster-General was responsible in Parliament for Government broadcasting policy and had substantial reserve powers, but he did not interfere in the ordinary running of the B.B.C.

The first attempts to establish a national grid for electricity supplies after 1918 failed,[10] and the Weir committee reported in 1926 in favour of a new authority to control generation and main transmission. This was accomplished by an Act passed the same year, and the Central Electricity Board began operation in 1927. The Board was appointed by the Minister of Transport after suggestions from various interested groups; but members had to sever all connection with bodies whose interests might conflict. It built and owned transmission lines, had full control of the main generating stations, and sold electricity to private and municipal distributors. Supervision was exercised by the Electricity Commissioners, but the Board was very largely autonomous in practice. In Parliament the establishment of the Board was supported by the Labour Party and criticised by some Conservatives as 'socialistic'. Nevertheless it was carried through by the Government as the only effective way of advancing the progress of the industry. Its monopolistic character made public responsibility desirable, but its independent management made it possible to combine this with business methods of operation, free from close political interference.

The reorganisation of public transport in London was a difficult and controversial matter. Since the beginning of the century, rising demand, lack of co-ordination and shortage of capital had prompted several mergers among the private-enterprise firms concerned. By the middle of the 1920s a combine, including the tube railways and most of the buses, had been built up under the control of Lord Ashfield. In 1928 a scheme for the co-ordination of London transport under private ownership was pressed forward. When Mr Herbert Morrison became Minister of Transport in the minority Labour Government of 1929, however, he decided on a policy of public ownership and unified control. Eventually an agreed scheme on these lines was negotiated with the existing undertakings, but the Labour Government fell before it could be enacted. With some modifications, however, it was put into effect by Liberal and Conservative ministers in the succeeding National Coalition Government.

The Act set up the London Passenger Transport Board. It consisted of seven members, who were appointed, not by the Government, but by a body of trustees — in fact, holders of important non-political public offices. The first chairman was Lord Ashfield, and an officer of the Transport Workers' Union was made a part-time member, after relinquishing union duties. The L.P.T.B. took over all buses, trolley buses, trams, tubes, and underground railways in London in July 1933, with monopoly powers and the object of providing an integrated service. The Board was financially independent, and supervision by either the Minister or Parliament was minimal.

With the establishment of these three bodies, the lines of the new type of institution were clear. The 'public service board', as it was usually called before the war, had emerged as an alternative public institution to the central department and the local authority. The challenging task—fundamental to public ownership of industry—of combining public responsibility with business-style management had begun.

The new corporations were essentially designed to meet particular circumstances, and for the Conservatives especially, who set them up, exceptional arguments were needed to justify the element of public ownership. Nevertheless, there was some theoretical commendation of these innovations. In 1926, in 'The End of *Laissez-faire*', J. M. Keynes noted that:

> ... In many cases the ideal size for the unit of control and organisation lies somewhere between the individual and the modern State. I suggest, therefore, that progress lies in the growth and the recognition of semi-autonomous bodies within the State—bodies whose criterion of action within their own field is solely the public good as they understand it, and from whose deliberations motives of private advantage are excluded ...[11]

In 1928 the Liberal Party issued its famous Yellow Book, entitled *Britain's Industrial Future*. This stressed the need 'to find room for various types intermediate between the Public and the Private Concern'. Existing public boards had crept into the system without sufficient criticism or consideration. Nevertheless, the ad hoc public board was a better model to follow than that of direct public trading.

Some other independent bodies, such as the Agricultural Marketing Boards and one other public corporation, the British Overseas Airways Corporation of 1939, were created by the pre-war Conservative-dominated Government. But in the end it was the Labour Party that was to make most use of the public corporation, and their acceptance of it deserves special attention.

It is convenient at this point, however, before turning to the Labour attitudes, to establish clearly what a public corporation is. There is much discussion of the 'theory of the public corporation' or the 'concept of the public corporation', and a summary of the main features of the institution will enable us to discern the issues more accurately.

(1) The term 'public corporation' describes a specific *legal* form, as public companies and industrial and provident societies are legal forms. The expression 'nationalised industry' is not a legal term. The public corporation is a corporate body—that is, it can trade in its own name, sue and be sued, own property, and so on.

(2) It is a statutory body; its constitution, powers and duties are prescribed by law and can be modified only by legislation.

(3) It is publicly owned; any securities it may issue give no powers of control to lenders and usually pay a fixed rate of interest.[12]

(4) There is some degree of Government control. This normally includes the appointment of a corporation's governing board, and may include by statute various policy and financial matters. In the post-war British nationalised industries the degree of control is considerable in practice.

(5) The corporation is independent in respect of its actual operations and management and has some degree of policy discretion. Its personnel are not civil servants, and its finances are separate from those of the Government.

There are in addition other practical rules that the British nationalised industries have in common—about pricing, accountability, finance, and so on. Most public corporations are financially autonomous in that they exist largely on trading revenue. The principle of Government-appointed boards excludes direct sectional representation. Out of the principles, however, some general themes emerge. The public corporation is disinterested in the sense that its controllers do not reap personal advantage from its activities; it does not operate for its own benefit, and it has no inherent self-regarding

C

motives for choosing one policy rather than another. Public
responsibility can be expected of it because it has no reason to evade it.

The dominant idea of the public corporation, however, is undoubtedly its combination of business management with public
accountability and control. It is on this combination that the concept
centres. It is here that the success of the public corporation, as a
distinct type of institution, must be judged. The proper phrase to
describe its administrative status is undecided: autonomous, semi-
autonomous, independent, semi-independent, and quasi-govern-
mental have all been used. Provided the principle is correctly
understood, they need not be misleading.[13]

In a democracy it is accepted that public institutions must ultimately be subject to popular control. For the public corporation
that control is exercised (whatever advisory or consultative arrangements there may be) only through the national machinery of
Government. It thus aims to be a system of *indirect* control by the
whole community, and not direct control by any sections of it.

The Labour Party and the public corporation

The creation of the public corporations between the wars, as just
described, was the work of Conservative or Conservative-dominated
Governments. Only in the planning of the London Passenger Transport Board did the Labour Party have any influence. It was not
clear, therefore, whether the public corporation was a suitable
instrument for nationalisation as the Labour Party envisaged it.
There were at least two reasons for suspecting that it might not be.
First, one of its main attractions for Conservatives was the possibility
of minimising political interference and applying the methods of
business management. The Labour Party, on the contrary, was
dedicated to industrial change by political means, and the idea of
making nationalised bodies as much like private business as possible
had no natural appeal. Secondly, the Labour Party was the party
of the trade unions and of employees generally. The new public
corporations gave the trade unions no share in industrial policy-
making and did nothing to modify the employer-employee relationship.

The objections to the public corporation's autonomy were the
first to be overcome. Members of the Labour Party had little faith
in the general run of businessmen, it is true; but they accepted that
some independent and experienced managers, freed from the profit
motive, would be of service. The alternative of control by Government departments was no great counter-attraction to the politically
minded, for the reputation of the Civil Service between the wars
was one of conservatism and timidity.

The place of the workers in a nationalised organisation, however,
took longer to settle, and it was discussed against a background of
industrial conflict in the 1920s which contributed to trade union
militancy. The situation in the coal industry led to a commission of
inquiry in 1919 under Sir John Sankey; and this, by a narrow
majority, recommended nationalisation. The trade unions proposed
to this commission that the mines should be owned by an independent Mining Council, with a minister as chairman. Half the
members were to be appointed by the Government and half by the
mineworkers' union. The plan thus embodied the doctrine of 'joint
control', and similar plans were put forward at various times in
the 1920s. In specifying an independent body, the miners had
clearly abandoned the idea of administration through a Government
department, but they were determined at this stage on sharing control themselves. The Minister's role in these plans — as a responsible
member of Government as well as a member of a council that
he could not control — was obscure, and his position probably un-
tenable.

It was not possible, in the event, to nationalise the mines at this
time, and the dispute in the industry led to direct action and the
General Strike of 1926. It was not until the early 1930s that the
question of the technique of nationalisation came to the forefront
again. By this time the Conservatives had established the British
Broadcasting Corporation and the Central Electricity Board.

In the 1929–31 Labour Government, which had no House of
Commons majority, the Minister of Transport was Mr Herbert
Morrison. In this capacity he was responsible for dealing with the
C.E.B., and he prepared legislation to reorganise London Transport

as just described. This was enacted, in a modified form, by the subsequent Conservative-dominated Government. (In general, Mr Morrison played a great part in persuading the Labour Party to accept the public corporation, as well as in helping to create several such bodies. In consequence there is a practice of referring to them as 'Morrisonian public corporations'.)

The absence of workers' participation in the management of the L.P.T.B. was therefore the occasion of renewed controversy in the Labour Party. The leader of the Transport and General Workers' Union, Mr Ernest Bevin, condemned the arrangements. At the 1932 Trades Union Congress a report which generally endorsed the idea of the independent public corporation was passed, but opposition from the T.G.W.U. led to the omission of the section that denied workers direct representation. In the same year Mr Bevin attacked the L.P.T.B. arrangements at the Labour Party Conference.

In the following years, however, agreement was reached on the necessary principles. The opponents of direct trade union representation pointed out that it would lead to pressure for other sectional representation, possibly from hostile groups. Management was becoming a highly skilled profession and should be as efficient as possible. The direction of big industrial concerns could not be carried on as a bargaining process between groups, and it was vital that nationalisation should be seen to be a success, or the public would lose faith in it. Moreover, the trade unions themselves would be placed in a false position if, because they were involved in management, they could not effectively represent the workers' interests. In the outcome of these arguments it became accepted that workers' participation would mean that some trade unionists would be appointed to management boards, and that the trade unions might suggest who these should be. But they would nevertheless be chosen by the Government and would retain no ties with their unions. They would not act as spokesmen for union policy. Instead, trade union views would be pressed through compulsory advisory and consultative machinery.

The settlement of this issue after 1935 meant that the main lines of nationalisation methods were decided. In principle, the Labour movement had accepted the public-corporation model recommended by the Liberals and initiated by Conservative Governments. There were some modifications in practice—such as the rights of trade unions to consultation, and more explicit powers of control by the Government—but the main structure of the new institutions was clear and widely accepted by all parties. A current of opinion in favour of more direct representation of workers in management has continued, but so far it has had no effect.

It should be remembered that in the 1930s and 1940s the Labour Party was much influenced by the ideas of economic planning previously mentioned. The public corporation seemed to fit the needs of planning in two ways. It embodied strong managerial authority, so that it could ensure that agreed central plans were carried out; and yet it was sufficiently independent to be able to respond to market pressures and so enable consumer demand to affect future plans. To some extent, therefore, the decline of ideas on workers' participation and joint control should be seen as consequences of the rising belief in the need for a centrally planned economy.

In retrospect, three main periods can be distinguished in Labour Party thinking about control of public enterprise. In the first, before the First World War, it was assumed (rather than explicitly argued) that the Government department, such as the Post Office, provided the model for a public enterprise. Secondly, in the 1920s joint control was favoured. Thirdly, the managerial public corporation was accepted, after argument, in the 1930s. The possibility of distinguishing a fourth period after 1955, when various other schemes were put forward, is discussed in Chapter 8.

3 The Major
Nationalised Industries

Most nationalisation as we now understand it dates from the years 1946–9.

As indicated in Chapter 2, there was by this time some growth of public ownership, partly associated with the new public corporations, partly with local authorities, and partly with other bodies. Thus public corporations of an industrial character existed in electricity and in London passenger transport. In 1939 an Act was passed setting up a new air-transport organisation, the British Overseas Airways Corporation, but the war prevented its coming into operation. There was much municipal enterprise that could be considered industrial. About one-third of the gas industry was in municipal ownership, and so were two-thirds of electricity distribution. City bus services were typically owned by local authorities. A few large towns had also begun to operate municipal aerodromes. Manchester shared the ownership of the Manchester ship canal, and Hull owned the local telephone system. Bristol owned docks, and Birmingham a municipal bank. The central Government operated industrial undertakings like naval dockyards, the Royal Ordnance factories, and the Royal Mint. The public houses of Carlisle and near-by districts had been Government-owned and managed since the First World War. With the growth of telephone and telegraph communications, the post office had become in part an engineering service. In 1938 the right to receive royalties on coal mined was transferred from the landowners to a public Coal Commission. In addition, of course, there were numerous non-industrial activities in public ownership, controlled directly or indirectly by the Government—from the British Broadcasting Corporation and the Forestry Commission to the Racecourse

Betting Control Board (running the totalisator) and the National Stud.

The war of 1939–45 diverted the normal progress of industrial organisation. In these years industry generally was subjected to a system of close control involving the rationing of scarce materials, the allocation and direction of labour, and in many industries the concentration of civil production in a limited number of firms. The railways were taken over and operated on behalf of the Ministry of War Transport. Road haulage, coastal shipping and canals were likewise closely controlled. But all these measures, drastic as they were, consisted of controls imposed without disturbing the existing ownership.

A few highly specialised firms—S. G. Brown Ltd (precision instruments), Power Jets Ltd (jet-propulsion engines), and Short Bros (aircraft)—ended the war in public ownership. The case of Short Bros was the most significant. The Government took the firm into public ownership in 1943 and then replaced the existing management by directors of its own choice. Even the powerful wartime controls were found inadequate and had to be surpassed in this case at least. But in the general story of wartime industry this was a mere incident.

Party programmes in 1945

This is not the place to analyse the causes of changes in political attitudes. It is important to note, however, that the reforms in the air at the end of the war were overwhelmingly of an economic character. By this time there had arisen a general popular demand for change in the economic system. The great evils of the inter-war years had been depression and unemployment; and no politician doubted that, somehow, they had to be conquered. The publication in 1936 of J. M. Keynes's *General Theory* provided a theoretical basis for controlling the economy, and in 1944 the Coalition Government published a White Paper making proposals on *Employment Policy* which embodied some of Keynes's ideas. There was in addition great political controversy at this time about social security, dominated by Sir William Beveridge's report on *Social Insurance and Allied Services* of 1943.

But underlying these discussions were more deep-seated political attitudes, and the parties made their responses to the needs of the period in accordance with philosophies shaped over many years. As we have seen, the Labour Party had long declared itself a socialist party, and though this meant many different things to different people, none in the Party doubted that measures of public ownership would be involved. The Conservative Party was not prepared to advocate any such measures. In the past it had carried through many schemes for the regulation of industry and had set up public corporations in special fields; and by 1945 it was ready for further economic and industrial reform. But nationalisation or other public ownership was regarded by Conservatives as unnecessary, bureaucratic, and possibly totalitarian.

The Labour programme for the 1945 election was called *Let us face the future*. It included a large variety of proposals — on planning for full employment, on social security, on housing — and it stated clearly:

There are basic industries ripe and over-ripe for public ownership and management in the direct service of the nation. There are many smaller businesses rendering good service which can be left to go on with their useful work.

There are big industries not yet ripe for public ownership which must nevertheless be required by constructive supervision to further the nation's needs . . .

In the light of these considerations, the Labour Party submits to the nation the following industrial programme:

1. *Public ownership of the fuel and power industries* — For a quarter of a century the coal industry, producing Britain's most precious national raw material, has been floundering chaotically under the ownership of many hundreds of independent companies. Amalgamation under public ownership will bring great economies in operation and make it possible to modernise production methods and to raise safety standards in every

colliery in the country. Public ownership of gas and electricity undertakings will lower charges, prevent competitive waste, open the way for co-ordinated research and development, and lead to the reforming of uneconomic areas of distribution. Other industries will benefit.

2. *Public ownership of inland transport* — Co-ordination of transport services by rail, road, air and canal cannot be achieved without unification. And unification without public ownership means a steady struggle with sectional interests or the enthronement of a private monopoly, which would be a menace to the rest of industry.

3. *Public ownership of iron and steel* — Private monopoly has maintained high prices and kept inefficient high-cost plants in existence. Only if public ownership replaces private monopoly can the industry become efficient.

These socialised industries, taken over on a basis of fair compensation, to be conducted efficiently in the interests of consumers, coupled with proper status and conditions for the workers employed in them.

An earlier passage in the manifesto stated:

... the Bank of England with its financial powers must be brought under public ownership, and the operations of the other banks harmonised with industrial needs.

And in the section on the land:

Labour believes in land nationalisation and will work towards it, but as a first step the State and the local authorities must have wider and speedier powers to acquire land for public purposes wherever the public interest so requires.

To the careful reader this indicated that land would not be nationalised, but that public authorities would have powers of compulsory purchase.

With these declarations in favour of public ownership as part of its programme, the Labour Party fought and won the General Election of 1945, under the leadership of C. R. Attlee.

THE PROCESS OF LEGISLATION

The Labour Government that took office in August 1945 was heavily occupied by general problems of demobilisation and reconstruction, the balance of payments, and social-service reform. There was, however, a feeling in the Party that the long-heralded opportunity given by its electoral success should not be missed. Other parties, and previous Labour minority Governments, had been accused of disappointing expectations, of betraying promises when power had been achieved. The feeling of the time, especially on the left, was that the least that could be done to avoid a repetition of such charges was to carry out the declared programme to the full.

At all events, nationalisation plans were not delayed. There seems to have been some rough order of priority in that the Bank of England (the simplest) and the coal industry (the most urgent) came first, and the steel industry (the most doubtful) was left until late — perhaps too late for its effective accomplishment. There was a Cabinet committee on the socialisation of industry, and the Cabinet committee on future legislation provided places for nationalisation measures in the long series of Government Bills that were carried through Parliament.

For most Bills a 'guillotine' motion was passed, providing a timetable for the committee stage, when detailed amendments could be considered. This practice limited discussion, and some clauses were passed through the Commons undebated; but it made sure that reasonable progress was achieved and that effective obstruction was not possible. The House of Lords, where the Conservative Party has a large permanent majority, acquiesced in nationalisation Acts, as it did in other Labour legislation, until the presentation of the Parliament Bill and the Steel Bill. Guided by Lord Salisbury, then Conservative Leader in the Lords, peers proposed amendments to legislation but did not insist on the acceptance of their views while, in their opinion, the mandate of the Labour Party held good.

In 1949 events took a different turn, as is explained below (pp. 56–8).

Most of the main Acts have a similar form. They begin by prescribing the position of the new corporation and its governing board, its powers, and duties. Then the terms of compensation are set out, followed by the financial arrangements of the new body. The principle of full compensation had been accepted, after some argument, by the Labour Party between the wars. The Acts provided for the compulsory replacement (usually at market value on a certain day) of existing stocks and shares by new fixed-interest stock, which carried no ownership rights but which could be bought and sold like other Government securities. The meeting of interest charges on this compensation stock became a statutory duty of the new corporations. The Acts also gave the relevant Minister the power to nominate the actual time of take-over. There was thus an interval of a few months between the final passing of an Act and 'vesting day', in which the first boards could be appointed and preliminary administrative arrangements made.

The Bank of England

The first nationalisation measure, the Bank of England Act, was passed by February 1946. This was a simple move designed to prevent the Bank from pursuing policies different from (and perhaps in opposition to) those of the Government. The assets were transferred to the Treasury, and the Court of Governors was reduced in size, but the structure of the Bank's organisation remained as before. Formal power of direction over the Bank, after consultation, was given to the Chancellor of the Exchequer; and the Bank in turn has power, with Treasury consent, to give directions to commercial banks. (Neither power has been used.) The existing Governor, Lord Catto, was reappointed and remained in office until 1949.

The independence of the Bank has remained a matter of some controversy. In 1957, during the controversies surrounding the Bank Rate Tribunal, critics alleged that the Bank of England was the effective source of monetary policy, and that it reflected the opinion of the City of London rather than that of the Treasury and the

Government. After the report of the Radcliffe Committee on the working of the monetary system in 1959,[1] some formal changes were made, but the realities of the situation remain. The Bank works with the Treasury but develops its own views, based on its contacts with industry and financial circles. The Government is legally in a position to impose its will, but normally the relationship is one of collaboration and consultation.

Coalmining

A much more significant step was taken in 1946 with the nationalisation of the coalmining industry. For many supporters of the Labour Party this lay at the centre of their plans and at the heart of their emotions. There was a long and bitter history of bad labour relations in the industry, and in many places the miners formed a closed community entirely dependent on the local pits. Industrial strife and economic depression had brought poverty and despair to these communities, and hence a feeling that not mere amelioration but a fundamental change in the order of things was required. Moreover, the years of depression had starved the industry of capital and of technical progress; and there had been insufficient reorganisation and amalgamation, in spite of Government attempts to promote them.

Mr Emanuel Shinwell, the Minister of Fuel and Power in charge of the Bill, complained afterwards[2] that he had only a few pamphlets and private memoranda to guide him in fashioning the new structure. But there were at least some preparatory ideas, from the Sankey Commission onwards: and one of the private memoranda had been drawn up by Mr Shinwell himself, with Mr John Strachey. In the event, the Coal Industry Nationalisation Act of 1946 set up a public corporation on lines foreshadowed by pre-war experience.

The case for the Bill, as presented, was more practical and less dogmatic than might have been expected. The sad state of the industry needed no elaboration. The technical failings of British coalmining had just been set out in the report of a Government committee under the chairmanship of Sir Charles Reid.[3] This did not actually recommend public ownership, but stressed the cardinal

necessity for 'a comprehensive scheme of reorganisation' under an
Authority which would ensure that the existing companies (whose
pattern was often ill suited to the mining of coal measures in
particular areas) were merged into effective units. Taken with the
general social situation in the coalfields, there was an overwhelming
incentive, for any Government not ideologically opposed to it,
to proceed with nationalisation. The Conservatives, who had some
grounds of principle for resisting public ownership, in fact criticised
particular points in the Bill and voted against it on the grounds that
it failed to solve specified problems of the industry. The Liberals
supported it, their Leader (Mr Clement Davies) declaring that it
would be 'one of the most epoch-making Acts of Parliament in our
history'.

The Act set up the National Coal Board, which, since vesting day
(January 1st, 1947), has owned all the mines in Great Britain. It
has a right to a monopoly of 'working and getting the coal', but
small mines may be operated by private enterprise under licence
from the Board. In 1964 there were about five hundred such mines,
and they accounted for one per cent of national coal production.
Coal distribution remains in private hands, except for some arrangements in the Midlands, where the old colliery companies had also
been distributors. In taking over the old companies, the Board also
acquired various ancillary activities, such as coke ovens and tar-
distillation plant, and enough brickworks to make it the country's
second largest producer. Compensation to the coal-owners was on
a 'net maintainable income' principle, not (as with later measures)
on Stock Exchange values.

The first Coal Board consisted of nine members under the
chairmanship of Lord Hyndley. The actual take-over was smoothly
effected, but the coal shortage in the very cold winter of 1947
brought early sharp criticism. Despite the establishment of divisions
and areas for administrative purposes under the Board, there were
many accusations of over-centralisation. A new Coal Industry Act
of 1949 increased the size of the Board and introduced part-time
members. The chairmanship of Sir Hubert Houldsworth (1951-5
was marked by strenuous efforts to raise production, but under

Sir James Bowman (1955–60) there was a check to demand that brought about large stocks of small coal. Further reorganisation was carried out after the Fleck report of 1955, discussed in Chapter 5. Lord Robens, the fourth chairman, has so far seen the industry in a more balanced and progressive condition than it has been for many decades.

Civil aviation

Before 1939, commercial air transport was in its pioneering days. Imperial Airways, a subsidised company, had opened many Empire routes, and British Airways, also subsidised, was doing the same in Europe. The Conservative Government amalgamated these into a publicly owned corporation just before the war. The technical progress of aviation during the war was enormous, but the total neglect of civil flying meant that a new start had to be made after 1945.

The Labour Government decided to continue the British Overseas Airways Corporation, nominally in existence, and to set up two new ones, British European Airways and British South American Airways, all being independent public corporations. These three were to be the only British airlines to provide regular services; but privately owned companies would be allowed a subordinate place.

In the main debate on the Bill, Labour spokesmen stressed that subsidies would be necessary at first to any airline, and that nationalisation by public corporation would enable these to be used effectively and without meddlesome supervision. The Conservatives criticised the monopolistic features of the plan—that is, the restrictions on the scope allowed to private-enterprise companies—and alleged that excessive powers had been given to the Minister. The Bill was passed as the Civil Aviation Act 1946.

In 1949 British South American Airways was merged with the British Overseas Airways Corporation. In 1952 the Conservative Government gave greater scope to private airlines, which in 1960 secured a major breakthrough by being made legally free to compete for providing any service, including regular scheduled services. In practice, however, no service can be operated without the permission of the Air Transport Licensing Board, and this body thus determines the opportunities open to the various operators. In February 1965 the Labour Minister of Aviation, Mr Roy Jenkins, indicated that the scope of services provided by independent airlines would be limited. Foreign airlines, of course, can obtain permission to fly on non-internal routes, and they provide the real competition for B.O.A.C.

There have been rumours from time to time (in 1953 and again in 1963) of unification of the two remaining corporations. But they provide very different services: B.E.A. is a 'short-haul' operator, and B.O.A.C. flies on long transatlantic, Commonwealth, and other world-wide routes. At the end of 1963, co-ordination between the two airlines was emphasised when the chairman of each line was made a member of the board of the other.

Nearly all civil airports providing regular services were owned and run directly by the Ministry of Aviation after the war, and Mr Herbert Morrison declared in 1946 that 'if ever there was a service which is not fit for municipal enterprise, it is the provision of airports.'[4] The growth of private-enterprise flying has encouraged the growth of the lesser airports, however, and there has been in fact considerable growth in municipal provision since 1955; this was accelerated in 1961, and in 1965 a British Airports Authority was created to run four main airports. Landing charges are made for use of airfields, and it is hoped that eventually airports will be financially self-supporting; at present they are subsidised by the central Government.

Aircraft construction is a private-enterprise industry, though the Royal Air Force and the nationalised airlines buy most of its output. In consequence the Government is in a strong position to deal with it, and in 1959–60 Mr Duncan Sandys, then Minister of Aviation, was able to impose drastic amalgamations. A committee of inquiry into the aircraft industry, under the chairmanship of Lord Plowden,[5] recommended in 1965 that the Government should purchase a financial share in the two largest construction companies, the British Aircraft Corporation and Hawker Siddeley; and a majority of the committee believed that this should be a majority holding, in order to give effective control.

Cable and Wireless

Cable and Wireless Ltd was a firm established in 1929 which operated various international telecommunication links, particularly between Britain and countries in the Commonwealth. In 1938 the British Government acquired a minority of the shares, in 1946 the Labour Government decided on the compulsory transfer of the rest, and this was achieved, under the Cable and Wireless Act, on January 1st, 1947. In 1948 the property of the company and its subsidiaries was divided among member-States of the Commonwealth.

Public ownership in this case has not meant the creation of a public corporation, and the usual forms of control and accountability do not apply. The company now operates foreign and Commonwealth communication services, and owns submarine cables and cable ships.

Transport

In some ways transport was better prepared for nationalisation than any other industry, and yet it has maintained a persistent air of crisis, punctuated by drastic reorganisations. Preparation was helped by the fact that the railways had been subjected to detailed Government regulation from the beginning, and in 1921 the system had been recast into four main companies by the Railways Act. Transport in London was unified under public ownership by the London Passenger Transport Act of 1933. His experience in the preparation of this Act inspired Mr Herbert Morrison to write *Socialisation and Transport*, thus providing the most considerable practical scheme of nationalisation to be prepared in advance. Road haulage was in private hands but controlled by a licensing system established by the Government in 1933. A high proportion of bus services were municipally owned; all were regulated by licence. The roads themselves, of course, are publicly owned; but no one has ever seen fit to administer them as part of the transport industry.

The Transport Act of 1947 was a nationalisation measure with a policy. The structure of the new public corporation was deliberately designed to bring about the integration of the country's transport.

That is to say, competition between the different *forms* of transport
(particularly between road haulage and the railways) was to be
minimised, and each type fitted into a unified system. The Act
itself did not bring this about directly, but it created the British
Transport Commission, a small board of five full-time members, for
the purpose; Lord Hurcomb, a former civil servant, was the first
chairman. The B.T.C. itself became the owner of all transport
property specified in the Act, and it had complete control over
policy. Nevertheless, the actual management of the undertakings
was in the hands of a series of Executives —a Railways Executive, a
Road Haulage Executive, a Road Passenger Executive,[6] a Docks
and Inland Waterways Executive, a Hotels Executive, and a
London Transport Executive. These comprised small boards
appointed by the Minister but regarded essentially as agents of the
Commission.

The proposals concerning road transport need further explanation.
Since 1933, goods transport by road has been controlled by a
system of licences —'A' and 'B' for haulage firms and 'C' for those
carrying only their own goods. The 1947 Act used the restrictions
possible through the operation of this system to check competition
against nationalised services. In particular, private road-haulage
firms (holding 'A' and 'B' licences) were confined within a twenty-
five-mile radius; and 'C'-licence vehicles were still forbidden to
work for hire. For road-passenger services the Commission was to
prepare schemes for specified areas which would co-ordinate the
services with one another and also with rail provision. Within this
framework the Commission would acquire but services and long-
distance road haulage – that is, the hauliers whose business was
predominantly over a forty-mile radius. Prices charged by the Commission would be supervised by a transport tribunal, described in
Chapter 6.

The Bill aroused a good deal of opposition, encouraged partly
by the railway companies and transport users, but pressed most
vigorously by the Road Haulage Association, representing the private
road-transport firms. Petitions against it were presented to the
House of Commons, and the R.H.A. advised its sympathisers:

D

On the morning of 17th December, without fail, send a
telegram to your Member as follows, Conservative, Liberal or
Socialist, condemning the Bill ... You should remember that
all Conservative M.P.s are on our side, and word your telegram, therefore, more politely to them than to the supporters
of the Government.

Pamphlets, films, posters, Press publicity, and other methods were
also used, and the whole campaign, polite and rude, cost £100,000.

In the Commons the Conservatives totally opposed the Bill. The
Liberals also decided against it, though they would have accepted
nationalisation of railways and canals in another form. Critics
condemned both the prospective lack of freedom for transport
users to choose their own form of transport, and the restrictions
placed on the use of a firm's own transport. There was also some
displeasure over the terms of compensation, and a Member quoted
The Economist's declaration that '. . . it is the widow and the orphan,
the patient and the pensioner, who will mainly suffer.'[7]

In spite of criticism and campaigns the Bill was passed, and the
Act received the royal assent in August 1947. The railways, canals,
and London Transport were taken over on vesting day (January
1st, 1948), but other parts of the industry were acquired gradually.
For several years the Commission was busy taking over road-
transport firms, both passenger and goods-carrying, and there was
slow progress in carrying out the policy of integration. In 1948 the
provincial bus group of Thos Tilling was acquired, and in 1949
that of Scottish Motor Traction. In addition, the Commission had a
minority shareholding in a holding company called British Electric
Traction Co. Ltd, which owns most of the private-enterprise bus
companies of any size. Road-haulage companies were also taken
over, and by 1952 the Commission owned 42,000 lorries.

Various other enterprises came into public ownership with the
Transport Act, often because they had been previously owned by
the railway companies, rather than out of deliberate policy. The
railway hotels form a substantial concern. Pickford's road services
and Carter Paterson road-parcels services are publicly owned, and

so are two well known travel agencies, Thomas Cook and Dean & Dawson. Docks owned by the railways came under the Commission. Shares in some shipping companies were also acquired.

Less than four years after nationalisation, the Conservatives came to power, with a different set of transport policies. They quickly called a halt to further acquisitions by the Commission, and they ended the integration policy. The 1952 annual report of the Commission sets out some projects that were abandoned. For example, the railways' collection-and-delivery services were to be combined with local services of the Road Haulage Executive; motor engineering and stores were to be unified; some road-haulage traffic was to be carried on rail trunk lines; and some cross-country rail parcels were to go by road.

Conservative policy was embodied in the Transport Act 1953. This first set out to denationalise long-distance road haulage; and it required the British Transport Commission to reorganise its administrative structure. The system of Executives was abolished, and the Commission's tasks of preparing co-ordination schemes and taking over docks and harbours were cancelled. The denationalisation of road haulage was no great success: it proved impossible to sell all the vehicles down for disposal, and in 1956 a further Act put a road-haulage organisation, British Road Services, on a permanent basis as a subsidiary of the British Transport Commission. An attempt to revive the railways largely by technical development was begun in the British Railways Modernisation Plan of 1955, at a cost of £1,660 million.

Continued financial difficulties of the railways led to further proposals by the Conservative Government in December 1960. After an unpublished report by a committee under Sir Ivan Stedeford, the Government decided to put an industrialist from the chemical industry, Dr Richard Beeching, in charge of a new drive for financial viability, replacing Sir Brian Robertson, who had been chairman in the years 1953–61. By the Transport Act 1962 the British Transport Commission was abolished and a British Railways Board set up, with great responsibilities transferred to regional railway boards.[8] Road haulage, road-passenger services, Cook's travel agency, and other interests were transferred to a holding company in public ownership; canals to a new British Waterways Board; and nationalised docks to a British Transport Docks Board. General transport supervision was retained only in the form of an advisory council to the Minister of Transport. At the new Railways Board Dr Beeching set out to achieve commercial success. A report on *The Reshaping of British Railways* in 1963 set out plans for doing so by introducing new freight services (liner trains); by closing many non-paying lines, and by other means; and another report in 1965, *The Development of the Major Railway Trunk Routes*, described proposals for streamlining trunk services. In 1965 Mr S. E. Raymond succeeded Dr Beeching as chairman.

The story of transport nationalisation is thus a complex one. In brief, however, it began with a grand structure aimed at achieving an objective, 'integration', never made completely clear. Before much progress had been made, political change brought a new philosophy of competition into operation, and the structure has been progressively broken up—though public ownership has been retained, part of road haulage excepted. Paradoxically, with the culmination of these policies in 1961–3, discussion of integration became fashionable again.

Electricity

The nationalisation of electricity was preceded by the report of a committee on electricity distribution (the McGowan Committee), which in 1936 recommended considerable amalgamation among the existing undertakings. The generation of electricity was already in the hands of the publicly owned Central Electricity Board, which operated the grid. It was clear that the need for electricity would rise considerably, and that there would be great economies from the use of larger power stations and general standardisation of methods. There was, therefore, a case for nationalisation on technical and organisational grounds.

In the debates in 1947 the Conservatives opposed the Bill on the grounds that it would cause great dislocation and that the position of consumers would be damaged. The Liberals voted for it.

As a result of the Act, the whole industry was owned and controlled by the British Electricity Authority (called the Central
Electricity Authority after 1955), though distribution was organised
by a number of regional boards. The whole system was reviewed
by an official committee, which in 1956 produced the Herbert
Report, one of the most important documents in the story of British
nationalisation.[9] The general implications of the doctrines advanced
in this report will be discussed later, particularly in Chapters 5 and
7. For electricity the consequence was the break-up of the unified
structure over which the first chairman, Lord Citrine, had presided
between 1948 and 1957. There are now twelve Area Electricity
Boards, concerned with distribution; a Central Electricity Generating Board (chairman, Mr F. H. S. Brown); and an Electricity
Council with certain general and supervisory duties (chairman,
Professor Sir Ronald Edwards). All these have an autonomous
statutory existence, and their members are appointed individually by
the Minister of Power.

In Scotland there are different arrangements. The 1947 Nationalisation Act excluded the North of Scotland from its general provisions, and this region was served by the North of Scotland
Hydro-Electric Board. This body had been established in 1943, and
in 1947 it was necessary only to modify its constitution slightly.
In 1954 the South of Scotland Electricity Board (which does not use
water power) was also made independent. Both are public corporations of the normal type, supervised by the Secretary of State for
Scotland, not the Minister of Power.

The post-war history of electricity has been marked by a steep
and steady rise in demand, and its main problem has lain in keeping
pace with growing requirements. Generation is now effected by
burning heavy oil as well as coal, and a tiny contribution is made by
nuclear power stations.

Gas

In 1948 the Labour Government began to nationalise the gas
industry. Again, there was a preceding inquiry by an official committee, resulting in the Heyworth Report of 1945.[10] This proposed

that regional boards, set up by Act of Parliament, should acquire all the undertakings in their own areas. Larger units in the industry were necessary, it claimed, to lower production costs, to develop research, sales, and distribution, and to eliminate inefficient plant.

The Bill provided for the transfer of all gas undertakings — whether municipally or privately owned — to twelve Area Gas Boards. Each Board has a monopoly of the manufacture and supply of gas within its boundaries; some ancillary activities — coking, tar distillation, and chemical by-products — were inherited from the companies taken over, but no attempt was made to acquire such activities deliberately. The Area Boards are appointed by the Minister and are the main management bodies of the industry. They are co-ordinated to some extent, however, by a Gas Council, which consists mainly of the chairmen of the Area Boards but also has a full-time chairman and vice-chairman. Its functions are concerned with research, training and education, the raising of capital, and the manufacture of plant or fittings. The structure of the gas industry is therefore decentralised — by the nationalisation statute itself — to a much greater extent than that of other nationalised industries.

The Bill was steered through the Commons by Mr Gaitskell, then Minister of Fuel and Power, against vigorous opposition. The Government argued, mainly on the lines of the Heyworth report, that larger units with pre-determined boundaries were necessary; and only nationalisation could ensure speedy action. The Conservatives suggested that nationalisation was unnecessary, and that (with coal and electricity) a dangerous fuel and power monopoly was being created. The Liberals supported the Bill.

There have been no major structural changes since nationalisation, though within the various Areas there has been much reorganisation and administrative rationalisation. Eventually the industry was able to achieve considerable technical progress. New methods of manufacturing gas, underground storage, the import of natural gas, and the provision of a trunk pipeline across England were projected in the 1960s. These advances made it necessary for the Gas Council to acquire new powers.

Steel

The story of the nationalisation and denationalisation of the iron and steel industry reflects a clash of principles more clearly than does any other major episode in post-war politics.[11] The Labour Party was sharply divided from Conservatives and Liberals on the issue; nationalisation was forced through against bitter and determined resistance; compromises were rejected; and it was reversed as soon as its opponents had power to do so.

Government intervention in the steel industry began in the 1930s. Technical progress had been lagging and investment was inadequate. The Government of the day agreed to give tariff protection provided that steps were taken to reorganise and modernise the industry. The Import Duties Advisory Committee, a body whose general duty was to decide tariff changes in the national interest, was thus given a supervisory role over the steel industry, in that it had to be satisfied that protection was being used to secure improved efficiency. A new trade association, the British Iron and Steel Federation, was set up, and machinery for collective policy-making by the industry was developed to a greater degree than in any other private-enterprise industry. During the war an Iron and Steel Control was established with full powers over production and distribution, with many of its personnel recruited from the B.I.S.F. The importance of steel in armament production made strict control of the allocation of supplies essential, and continued shortage relative to demand meant that steel rationing was needed for many years after the war. In 1946 an interim system of public control was established through an Iron and Steel Board, which comprised two independent members (including the chairman), two employers, two trade unionists, and a representative of steel-using firms.

However, the steel industry had been scheduled for nationalisation in 1945 in *Let us face the future*. The leaders of the steel industry were prepared to accept strong public control, and they hoped that a system could be arranged which would satisfy the Labour Party without entailing full public ownership. Private discussions between the industry and members of the Government took place in the summer of 1948, and a tentative agreement was reached with Mr Herbert Morrison. The idea of compromise did not please many Labour politicians, however, and the agreement (whose contents are still secret) was not accepted by the Cabinet.[12]

The decision of the Government to proceed with nationalisation brought many problems. Relations with the industry deteriorated rapidly and its representatives on the Iron and Steel Board withdrew, making the work of that body impracticable. Vehement political opposition was aroused, and the Conservative majority in the House of Lords seemed likely to show its strength at last and reject the Bill. Moreover, the iron and steel industry was a very complex one with many ramifications, and the technique of nationalisation was more difficult to apply than before.

The Government tried to forestall the action of the House of Lords with a new Parliament Act. The first Parliament Act of 1911 had limited the powers of the Lords, so that they could delay legislation for only two years. The new proposal shortened the delay to one year. The Lords opposed this curtailment, and so the Bill had to be passed under the terms of the 1911 Act.

The Nationalisation Bill proposed the setting up of a public corporation, the Iron and Steel Corporation of Great Britain, but this would not manage the industry directly. The existing companies would retain their identity, the ownership of their shares being transferred to the Iron and Steel Corporation, which would achieve control through the operation of ordinary company law. Only those companies were to be acquired which were predominantly concerned with steel production. In fact, some steel is produced by firms (in the engineering and other industries) who are mainly concerned with other things. Thus, for example, on nationalisation in 1951, twelve per cent of tinplate, twenty-seven per cent of cold rolled strip, and eighty per cent of bright steel bars were being turned out by these 'integrated' firms. Consequently, the Iron and Steel Corporation could never control the whole of Britain's steel production, and the unnationalised sector was sufficiently significant for it to be argued that other, wider machinery was necessary to plan on a national basis. The iron-foundry industry was not involved in the nationalisation project; iron-ore mining in England was almost entirely nationalised.

The Nationalisation Bill had a stormy passage through Parliament, guided by the Minister of Supply, Mr George Strauss. In its support the Government argued that it had a mandate to carry it, derived from the 1945 election manifesto, *Let us face the future*. The growth of policy-making through the British Iron and Steel Federation had made the industry, effectively, a monopoly. Methods of control and supervision had proved inadequate, the Government claimed, and neither the efficiency nor the capacity of the industry was all it should be. Steel was inescapably a basic industry, vital to the rest of the economy: it was right, therefore, that the Government should take full responsibility for it.

The Opposition denied all these contentions. Whatever the Party manifesto had said, there had been little mention of steel during the 1945 campaign. There was considerable competition in the industry, which was efficient and progressive. Moreover—and here there was a sharp clash of principle—this was not a public utility but a manufacturing industry; its labour relations were good; and there had been no official inquiry recommending reorganisation. The motives for nationalisation, alleged the Conservatives, were clearly political and ideological, and they felt justified in resisting the progress of the measure as vigorously as they could.

The fact that the controversy centred on the appropriateness of public ownership as such, rather than on the reconstruction or rehabilitation of the industry, accounted for much of its bitterness. Yet there were (and are) two other important elements. First, there was the 'planning' or 'effective control' argument against nationalisation, already mentioned: the absence of any public-corporation control of steel production in the (unnationalised) integrated firms made it a weak instrument for planning some parts of the industry. Secondly, for public ownership, there was the 'capacity' argument: as an industry on which many others rely, steel should have sufficient productive capacity to meet rising demand, and demand at the peak of a boom; otherwise it will constitute a bottleneck for economic expansion. But private ownership makes firms over-careful about profits and hence reluctant to risk idle capacity, which raises costs. Firms in the industry have therefore preferred a cautious level of expansion, prudently enough for them as private business, but hampering the steel-using industries and restricting efforts at national economic expansion.

The Bill passed the Commons after fierce debates and a committee stage where progress was made possible by a rigid timetable imposed by the Government. In the House of Lords the Conservative majority allowed the Bill to pass its second reading, but made many amendments in committee, most of which the Government's majority in the Commons refused to accept. The Conservative peers, guided by Lord Salisbury, declared their intention to insist on one amendment only: postponement of the actual take-over of the industry until after the next General Election. The Government were not at first disposed to accept this, but eventually it became clear that the industry could not in practice be transferred much sooner. The Bill was therefore amended so that vesting day could not be before the latest possible date for the General Election, and it was thus passed into law.

The Labour Party won the General Election of February 1950 by a very small majority. In spite of this, it declared its intention to implement the Act, and it began to make the necessary administrative arrangements. The leaders of the steel industry and the Conservative Party refused to resign themselves to nationalisation, however: they felt that the Government's majority was so slender and its prospects so insecure that delay might still bring some success. No prominent businessmen in the steel industry agreed to serve with the new Iron and Steel Corporation, and any steel industrialist who consulted the B.I.S.F. about service with the corporation was advised not to join it. In other words, the existing managers of the industry boycotted the new structure.

On February 15th, 1951, the industry passed into public ownership, and the Iron and Steel Corporation began its work under the chairmanship of Colonel Steven Hardie, who had previously been chairman of the British Oxygen Co. Ltd. Nevertheless, no immediate change took place in the management of the companies, who continued to consult together and to co-ordinate policies in their trade association, the British Iron and Steel Federation. The corporation made some changes in the boards of directors of the companies, and prepared consolidated accounts. Eventually its legal authority must have prevailed.

In October 1951, however, there was another General Election, and the Labour Government fell. The new Conservative Minister of Supply, Mr Duncan Sandys, issued a general directive under Section 4 (1) of the Act, prohibiting further changes in the industry's financial or management structure. In February 1952 Colonel Hardie resigned as chairman of the corporation after a confused dispute with the Minister about steel prices. Progress by the nationalised corporation was at an end, and in 1953 the Conservatives passed the Iron and Steel Act providing for the denationalisation of the industry.

This abolished the Iron and Steel Corporation and set up a regulatory Iron and Steel Board with functions relating to raw materials, prices, and industrial development. The actual ownership of the steel companies passed to the Iron and Steel Holding and Realisation Agency, a small, independent body with the duty of selling the companies to private owners. Preference has been given to previous owners of steel shares willing to buy, but many have been sold to the public. In its first five years ISHRA succeeded in disposing of most of the companies on its hands, regrouping some units and reorganising the structure of the stock in the process. But the process has since slowed down, and in 1964 one very large company (Richard Thomas & Baldwins Ltd) and a number of smaller enterprises remained with ISHRA. Ten years after the denationalisation Act, that is to say, they remained in public ownership.

In 1959 some substance was given to the Labour Party's contentions about the inadequate expansion of the industry. Following criticisms by the Iron and Steel Board of the development plans put forward by the companies, the Government authorised special loans of £120 million to two firms, Richard Thomas & Baldwins and Colvilles, to build new continuous-strip-rolling mills. The question of location (in order to provide employment in South

Wales and Scotland) was important, as well as that of the future capacity of the industry, and it was demonstrated that means of securing expansion—admittedly highly controversial ones—could be found without nationalisation.

The question of steel nationalisation remains politically alive. The Labour Party declared that it would renationalise at the time of the Conservative Act of 1953, and it has reaffirmed its intention to do so in several subsequent policy statements. When it returned to office in 1964, the Labour Party prepared new plans for the industry, and these were published in a White Paper on *Steel Nationalisation* in April 1965.[13] A national steel corporation would take over fourteen large companies, which in practice dominated the industry (they were responsible for over ninety per cent of most of its major products). The Iron and Steel Board was to be abolished, and whole-industry planning was to be fitted into the national system by means of an advisory committee.

Common characteristics

It is worth noting some features that the various nationalisation Acts had in common. First and most obviously, with minor exceptions they all set up public corporations on the model described in Chapter 2. There were no concessions either to workers' control or to direct administration by Government departments.

Secondly, the Acts contained stronger provision for control by ministers over the corporations than did pre–1939 legislation. A clause giving the relevant minister power to issue 'directions of a general character' was included in all post-war Acts but in none of the earlier ones. Again, the later Acts gave ministers the power to dismiss members of the boards (except for that of the Bank of England), and their period of office is a maximum, not a fixed, one. Powers of ministers to intervene in the financing of the corporations are also stronger in post-war legislation.

Thirdly, all the Acts made some provision for the representation of consumers—by establishing special councils or committees for the purpose. (These bodies are discussed in Chapter 6.) The boards were also obliged by all the Acts to establish machinery with the unions for settling pay and conditions, and to set up machinery for 'joint consultation' on matters affecting the industry generally.

Fourthly, all the Acts made similar statements about the obligation of corporations to cover their costs 'taking one year with another'. The elaboration of doctrine around this principle will be considered in later chapters.

Finally, the detail in which the structure of the corporations was set out in the Acts increased between 1946 and 1949. This may have been due to a desire to ensure decentralised organisation, but it also relates to the character of the various industries.

The Acts make it clear that public corporations have no power to commit unlawful acts, although they have wide freedom to pursue any activities that seem to them helpful to their duties. The corporations pay taxes in the same way as other businesses, and local rates in accordance with the arrangements for industrial and transport properties.

OTHER NATIONALISATION

The account given so far in this chapter excludes many public corporations and other government trading bodies.

A number of additional moves towards public ownership were made by the Labour Government. The centralised buying of supplies for the cotton industry begun during the war was continued by the Raw Cotton Commission, set up under the Cotton (Centralised Buying) Act of 1947. This was repealed by the Conservatives in 1954 and the market in cotton futures in Liverpool restored. The Licensing Act of 1949 provided for the State management of public houses in the new towns, but no progress had been made when the Conservatives repealed this provision in 1952.

By the Overseas Resources Development Act of 1948, two public corporations were set up—the Overseas Food Corporation and the Colonial Development Corporation. The first sponsored the ill-fated scheme to produce vegetable oils by growing ground-nuts in undeveloped areas in Africa, and it was wound up in 1955. The C.D.C. finances, preferably in collaboration with other bodies, a variety of projects for which capital cannot be found elsewhere.

The White Fish Authority (1951) and the Herring Board (1935) are public corporations that regulate and support the sea-fishing industry, which is not publicly owned. The Sugar Board is a public financial agency for subsidising and regulating the British Sugar Corporation.

The Town and Country Planning Act of 1947 embodied an attempt to nationalise the development rights in land. Following the recommendations of the Uthwatt committee in 1942, landowners were to be paid compensation for sacrificing their right to receive the 'betterment' that arose from development. When land increased in value through development – e.g. when its use was changed by permission of the planning authorities – the State would claim the betterment from the developer. The compensation provisions did not work, and the attempt at public ownership of these rights was abandoned by the Conservatives in 1953.

A full catalogue of Government bodies engaged in trade, and of public corporations and public authorities regulating or supervising industry, would be long and tedious. Its presentation would emphasise the variety as well as the extent of the Government's economic activities, and it is important to appreciate the many-sided character of the Government's concern.[14] But for the aspects of the subject dealt with in this book, the dominant role of the public corporations in the basic industries is clear. For the most part, therefore, succeeding chapters will concentrate their attention on the coal industry, the electricity industry, the gas industry, the railways and other inland transport, and the airlines. These fall into two groups, the power industries and transport, and three Government departments are mainly concerned – the Ministry of Power, the Ministry of Transport, and the Ministry of Aviation.

First, however, the position of three further public authorities deserves special explanation. These are the National Research Development Corporation, the Atomic Energy Authority, and the Post Office.

The National Research Development Corporation is perhaps a special case. It is a public corporation set up by the Development of Inventions Act 1948, and though clearly not an 'industry' in the usual sense, it was noted in the Labour Party's programme of 1961, *Signposts for the Sixties*, as a possible channel for the encouragement of further public ownership. Its role so far has been to examine new inventions and to consider their value for development and commercial exploitation. Some of these arise in Government or Government-sponsored research, and it may be inconvenient for the discoverers to pursue them further. The N.R.D.C. tries to arrange for them to be carried forward by other bodies, and it eventually offers them for commercial use. It also investigates the merits of inventions submitted to it by the public, and tries to ensure that no chance is lost of putting these to practical use: that is, in suitable cases it again tries to arrange further development and commercial application. It can help with finance for these purposes. The corporation consists of ten members — scientists, industrialists and financial experts. It is financed by loans from the Government and by royalties on the patented inventions it has made available to industry.

The N.R.D.C. does not itself originate research projects. Its function is to make sure that, as far as possible, no innovation that is commercially viable is suppressed, ignored, or neglected. Among the projects it has helped to promote are the Hovercraft, 'dracones' (long flexible containers for towing oil across the sea), printed electrical circuits, and the Cephalosporin antibiotic drugs, which are likely to have important uses in conditions where penicillin is not effective.

Atomic energy

The atomic-energy industry differs in many ways from the other nationalised concerns. It is a completely new industry and has never been run by private enterprise. Its origins lie entirely with the wartime developments that began in Britain and led to the construction in the United States of the first atomic bombs. For many years all atomic-energy projects were carried out under direct Government control, through the Department of Scientific and Industrial Research and the Ministry of Supply.

Since the war there have been two sides to the atomic-energy programme: first, the development and manufacture of nuclear weapons; and secondly, the furtherance of civil uses of atomic energy. The principal application on an industrial scale has been the building of power stations for the generation of electricity. Both sides of the programme are sustained by the Atomic Energy Research Establishment at Harwell, in Berkshire, set up in 1946.

By the Atomic Energy Authority Act of 1954, the Conservative Government transferred management to a new public corporation. This move was opposed by the Labour Party at the time, on the grounds that the arrangements would be cumbersome, and that atomic energy was so vital that direct Government responsibility was needed. The Authority consisted at first of five full-time and five part-time members; the numbers have varied slightly since. It has extensive powers over the whole field of atomic energy. Since 1964 it has been under the supervision of the Ministry of Technology.

There are thus three features that distinguish atomic energy from the other nationalised industries. First, it was not nationalised as part of the great Labour programme of 1946–9, and its public-corporation form is due to Conservative action. Second, though it manages its own finances, most of its income is derived from public funds, and its accounts are similar to those of Government departments. It provides power stations (for the Central Electricity Generating Board)[15] and nuclear weapons (by contract with the Ministry of Aviation), and it sells isotopes and some other products, but it is very far from being a commercial body. With this financial dependence goes close policy control by the Government. Third, much of its activity is still secret, and its employees, like civil servants, are subject to the Official Secrets Acts.

The industrial progress of atomic energy has been bedevilled by economic difficulties. At first it was hoped that electricity generated by nuclear stations would be cheaper than that from conventional (principally coal-fired) ones. But for many years it was in fact much more expensive. The capital cost of a nuclear power station is still several times that of a conventional one, and only in the latest designs is the cost of electricity generation down to that of conventional stations.

The Post Office

Postal and associated services constitute one of the most substantial of any modern government's trading services. The British Post Office can trace its origin to the sixteenth century, and in the nineteenth century its activities underwent a great expansion with the introduction of cheap postage. In 1869 the inland telegraph service was nationalised (probably the first use of the word), and in 1912 the telephone service was taken over completely, apart from the local-authority system in Hull. The Post Office also operates a banking service, set up in 1861, and acts as an agency for other Government services, such as the payment of old-age pensions.

Up to 1933 the Post Office was run like any other Government department. Since then there has been a series of changes, culminating in the Post Office Act of 1961.[16] The finances of the Post Office are now entirely separate from those of the rest of the Government and are reported to Parliament by commercial accounts only. Like the public corporations, it must try to ensure that its revenues cover its costs 'taking one year with another' — though to do this means that unprofitable services (such as telegrams) must be supported by the others. Investment is financed through the Exchequer and subject to control on economic grounds like that of other nationalised concerns, and a target for return on capital has now been fixed. The staff of the Post Office are still civil servants, and the Postmaster-General is a member of the Government, answerable to Parliament like other ministers.

The result of these changes is that the Post Office has become more like the industrial public corporation. But it is still a Government department and seems likely to remain one, for there are strong pressures to maintain mail-carrying as a direct Government responsibility, to keep parliamentary control, and to retain the present status of Post Office workers.

Nationalisation abroad

The amount of nationalisation in other countries varies enormously, since it lies at the heart of the great political issues of the century. In Communist countries, of course, virtually all enterprise

E

is publicly owned, though the system of direction and management bears little resemblance to the public-corporation method. There are wide variations in the amount of nationalisation in more comparable countries, reflecting their political temper in recent years.

France offers the greatest similarities to Britain. Railways were nationalised in 1936, and the coal mines, electricity, gas, the Bank of France, and some other banks were all nationalised in the post-liberation period 1944-6, in an even sharper burst than the British process. In addition, about half the French insurance business is publicly owned; and some enterprises (the Renault motor firm, for example) were nationalised because their owners had collaborated with the Germans during the war. Since 1948, Air France has been a company in which the Government holds the majority of shares.

The major enterprises form distinct concerns similar to our public corporations, but the direction of each has been put in the hands of a tripartite body. These boards consist of representatives of the personnel, of consumers, and of the Government, all serving part-time. There have been difficulties in working this system, partly because many board members are Communists who do not co-operate easily with the others, and partly because there is an inherent conflict between the groups represented. In consequence, these boards have found their position gradually weakened, and much power has passed to the ministries that supervise them and to the full-time professionals who manage them.

In Western Germany there is less public ownership, though the railways have long been nationalised, and there is much public enterprise in gas and electricity. For many years after the war the Volkswagen car firm had no shareholders and seemed to thrive without them, though a measure of private ownership has now been instituted.

Western Germany has experimented with another approach to industrial control—*co-determination*. Under the law of May 1951, which applies to the steel and coalmining industries, each firm in these industries has two-tier control: there is a supervisory council and a managing board. On the supervisory council there are five representatives of the shareholders, five of the employees, and one public figure chosen by these ten; and the council appoints the managing board. Members of the management cannot be members of the council, though they may attend its meetings. The law of October 1952 on the constitution of the enterprise applies to other industries. All firms with more than five employees must have a works council, with from three to thirty-five members. These systems mean that the control of German enterprise is closely regulated by law, but there is no direct ministerial supervision as with Britain's public corporations.

Italy has publicly owned railways, gas, and some other enterprises. Two large organisations (the Instituto per la Ricostruzioni Industriale and the Ente Nazionale Idrocarburi) act as publicly owned holding companies with shares in many firms, sometimes amounting to a controlling interest and sometimes not. In Scandinavia and the Low Countries there is rather less nationalisation than in the other three.

In all countries mentioned, telecommunications and railways are publicly owned, and there is some degree of public ownership in the fuel and power industries. Iron and steel are publicly owned in Austria and to some extent in Norway and Sweden. Many other industries are involved, including such goods as cigarettes (France), tobacco (West Germany) and matches (both). In many countries the State participates in business through joint enterprises, and a wide variety of industries are affected in this way.

The United States of America maintains private enterprise in fields where most other countries have abandoned it: airlines, railways, radio and television, and even telephones are all privately owned. Nevertheless, there is considerable public intervention, through independent regulatory agencies and otherwise. The Tennessee Valley Authority was established in 1933 as an agency 'clothed with the power of government, but possessed of the flexibility and initiative of a private enterprise', according to President Roosevelt. It has been largely responsible for the development of a whole region, based on hydro-electric and other power installations.

Though the degree to which Western countries have adopted

nationalisation varies, there are similarities in the general pattern. British nationalisation is comparatively extensive in the basic industries, sometimes called the 'infrastructure' of the economy. It is not particularly widespread in other industries, where there are comparatively few examples of publicly owned firms or special monopolies.

4

The Practice of
Nationalisation

Britain has now had over fifteen years' experience of nationalisation. There have been important changes and some considerable recasting of the structure of the corporations in that time, as described in Chapter 3. In this chapter the aim is to describe some of the main features of the experience of the various corporations. It is not possible to give economic or technical analyses of the progress of the industries in any detail. This book considers the problems of nationalisation as such, and the economics of power or of transport need separate treatment. It is necessary, however, even for those whose main interest is in politics and administration, to have some understanding of the industrial record of the corporations. This chapter therefore sets out some of the facts about their performance.

It will not be possible, here or elsewhere, to answer questions about the general 'success' of nationalisation. There is no obvious criterion of success; possible tests are vague and disputed, and in the past even the economic standards laid down by the Government were far from clear. It should also be borne in mind that the corporations have not been free agents. These questions of control and objectives are discussed in Chapters 6 and 7. Here there is a brief survey of major developments.

Financial affairs

The overall financial record of an organisation provides the most general summary of its activities, but not always the most revealing one. At one time the sole purpose of industrial activity was considered to be profit, and though now most enterprises acknowledge a multiplicity of objectives, financial viability is a prerequisite for achieving them. For public corporations there are special rules about financial behaviour.

The nationalisation Acts all stipulated that the public corporations were to cover costs taking one year with another—though there is no bankruptcy or other necessary consequence if they fail to do so. This standard was thought of mainly as a means of avoiding large profits or subsidies: since the corporations had considerable mono-polistic advantages, it was hardly doubted that the standard could be maintained. In fact, most of the corporations have made losses from time to time, and some of them considerable losses for long periods. The situations in the various industries, therefore, must be explained.

The National Coal Board has made a loss in many years of its existence, and particularly large ones in 1947, 1955 and 1959–61. Not until 1963 did it seem to have achieved a stable basis for its profitability. By then its accumulated deficits amounted to some £92 million.

The orthodox response of a trading concern to losses is to adjust either its selling prices or its costs and output, in order to remove them. The price of coal has been raised considerably since 1946, but rises have been delayed or limited, for national economic reasons, and deficits thereby incurred. Up till about 1956 there was such a shortage of coal that higher prices would not have checked sales very much, and so the Board could have improved its financial position if it had been permitted to charge more. Since then there has been an abundant supply of coal, competition from fuel oil for many uses has been severe, and the Board's prices have therefore been limited by market conditions. In the earlier period, moreover, the Board was pressed to secure maximum output, and at that stage it was obliged to continue producing coal from high-cost pits. After 1956 there was a period when costs were raised both by the building up of large stocks of small coal and because the Board had to meet the same 'standing charges' (the general overheads of the industry) from a smaller volume of sales. In 1965 it was announced that in view of the reduced capacity of the coal industry, its capital debt would also be reduced, and about £400 million (out of £1,000 million) of the Board's debt to the Exchequer was written off by the Government. The Government also made special funds available to assist industrial developments in areas affected by pit closures.[1]

Large losses have been made by nationalised transport, especially British Railways. For its first three years the British Transport Commission made considerable losses; from 1951 to 1953 there were surpluses, which then turned again to large losses. In 1956 the financial crisis had to be met by legislation. The Transport (Railway Finances) Act authorised advances by the Government up to a limit of £250 million to enable the B.T.C. to meet its deficits. At the same time a modernisation plan, described later in this chapter, was put in hand in order to make the railways—the principal cause of the Commission's difficulties—an up-to-date and profitable concern. Nevertheless, by 1960 the British Transport Commission was losing £100 million a year, of which £60 million was lost on the railways' running costs alone. In 1961 the reorganisation of nationalised transport embodied a drastic financial reconstruction: £400 million of debt were written off, £800 million put in 'suspense account', and the Treasury took responsibility for British Transport stock. The increasing rate of loss on British Railways was checked in 1963, when the annual deficit fell by £17 million to £87 million, in spite of increased costs.

The financial difficulties of the railways are of a long-standing nature. Most of the main-line railway companies have failed to make profits and pay dividends in many years between the wars. Until changes were made in 1956 and 1961, they operated under many restrictions devised when they had a monopoly of speedy transport: their charges had to be submitted to a statutory tribunal, which habitually made cuts in their proposals without giving reasons; they had to publish their scales of charges and thus could not discriminate between customers; and as a 'common carrier' they were obliged to transport all goods whether convenient to them or not. In short, they were expected to provide a public service. The financial circumstances of the railways in the 1950s made it finally clear that they could no longer provide a service on such a scale without major revisions of policy, and the controversies of the 1960s are directed towards shaping these new policies.

Other transport activities have not shared in the financial disasters of the railways. Inland waterways have made losses in most years, but other undertakings have in the main been financially self-supporting.

The secondary fuel industries have not been in serious financial trouble. There was a loss on electricity generation before 1950 but not since; and taken together the Area Boards concerned with distribution made a loss only in 1951–2. The Gas Boards together have not made a loss since 1950, though some have done so in particular years, and the Scottish Area Board had an accumulated deficit of about half a million pounds in 1963.

The nationalised airlines were in deficit and had to be subsidised during their early years, as foreseen when they were set up. B.O.A.C. made surpluses in the middle 1950s, but serious losses returned in 1957–8. By 1963 there was an accumulated deficit of £80 million. B.E.A. made surpluses after 1955 until 1961, and in 1963 it still had an accumulated deficit of £2½ million. The airlines found that the transition to large jet aircraft brought economic difficulties; some types of aircraft, such as the Britannias and early Comets, had special trouble. Both airlines have had non-commercial elements in their policies — some routes have been flown for prestige or social reasons, and there has been preference for British-built aircraft. In March 1965 it was announced that B.O.A.C. debts totalling £110 million would be written off. International air fares are regulated by agreement through the International Air Transport Association.

When the surpluses or losses of nationalised industries are considered, the method of calculation should be borne in mind. Compensation stocks are a statutory charge on the corporations, and the interest paid is reckoned as part of their costs. Some enterprises, such as B.E.A., started from scratch and do not have this burden of compensation; and the railways' obligations have been taken over by the Exchequer. The payments, in any case, are not in principle an unfair burden, for all industries must pay for their capital in some way. In private industry, however, dividends are paid out of profits, and are not usually regarded as costs. The logic of the method of presentation is plain in either case, but the differences should not be ignored.

An obvious factor affecting the finances of a corporation is its price policy. There are many facets to this topic, some of which will be discussed in Chapters 6 and 7. But in very few cases have public corporations been able to charge what they would do on commercial grounds. The statutory obligation to break even does not forbid profits, but it clearly does not envisage them on any large scale, and it has discouraged some industries from exploiting monopoly advantages when they could do so; there has been Government pressure to keep down prices to check inflation; there was the Transport Tribunal; and there is the international agreement on air fares. The upshot of these restrictions—often economically sound in isolation—has been that industries which got into difficulties found it very difficult to get out of them.

Comparisons of actual price movements between industries are extremely difficult to make and rarely have any validity. Since prices rise in steps, the period chosen for comparison may be crucial —a period starting just after a large rise and ending just before another one will show an extremely flattering result for a particular industry. There are usually many complicating factors, such as changes in tariff structure, as in electricity, or changes in the quality and nature of the product—coal now has to be obtained from deeper mines, and is more extensively processed to meet modern requirements. Most important, prices reflect not only costs and efficiency, but also changes in policies about industrial finance. It is often pointed out that loss-making by a nationalised industry means that it has to be supported by the taxpayer. While this is so, it should also be stressed that the losses are evidence that the consumer, directly or indirectly, has been getting the benefit of below-cost prices.

Investment

One of the main factors in the financial position of a nationalised industry is the size of its investment programme.

At the time of nationalisation many of the industries were in a backward condition, either generally or in part. The need to revive them was one of the main arguments for Government action, and it made nationalisation acceptable to many non-socialists.

The scale of finance necessary for investment is therefore very large. At first it was thought that money could be raised by borrowing in the usual way, at least for some industries. The Government and other public authorities habitually borrow very large amounts 'through the market', by issuing stock and otherwise. Since the purchase of this type of security carries no voting rights, lenders to a nationalised industry are not in the position of shareholders, and the principle of public ownership is unimpaired. Early public corporations, including the Central Electricity Board and the London Passenger Transport Board, raised capital in this way, under Government supervision.[2]

In the post-1945 corporations two Government controls on investment were prescribed by statute. First, major investment plans must have Government approval, on their economic merits. Second, borrowing to finance investment must have Government consent. The Acts permit varying ways of raising loans for the industries, but the Government is always involved. There is also a statutory limit to the total amount that each corporation may borrow. When this limit is reached, legislation to raise it is necessary, thus providing Parliament with an opportunity for debate and control.

With the exception of the National Coal Board, the post-1945 corporations began by borrowing from the market with the support of a Treasury guarantee. The N.C.B. received investment funds through the Ministry of Fuel and Power. For the others, the existence of the Treasury guarantee ensured that if private subscription to their issues of stock fell short, then the Exchequer would support them. The large sums needed during the 1950s made this the case on many occasions.

In 1956 the Chancellor of the Exchequer, Mr Harold Macmillan, decided to simplify the system by providing for all borrowing by the nationalised industries to be done through the Exchequer. This enables the Treasury to take a considered view of the borrowing situation and to avoid having to meet sudden situations by inconvenient means that interfere with its other money-market operations. It borrows on its own credit, that is to say, in convenient ways and at convenient times, and then in turn meets the needs of the national-ised corporations. Though this system was introduced as a temporary measure, the size of the requirements is so large that reversion to market-borrowing by the corporations has proved impracticable, and this will probably remain the situation. An interesting develop-ment in 1965 was the provision in the Air Corporations Act whereby part of the Government loan to B.O.A.C. would earn, not fixed interest, but a sum varying with the size of the profits—in other words, a payment akin to dividends on shares.

A further source of funds is, however, likely to increase in importance. Many private-enterprise firms retain a high proportion of their profits, so that they can finance much of their own invest-ment and do not have to appeal to the public for funds. Since 1961 it has been recognised that nationalised industries might do the same. They now adjust their price and sales policies so that a part of their investment can be paid for from their own reserves. The amount that can be financed in this way varies from industry to industry, and the need for Exchequer finance on a large scale will continue for many years.

Investment, whatever its source, is expected to yield a return. The size of this return has recently been made explicit for most of the corporations: it varies from industry to industry, usually in the region of six to eight per cent on the value of their net assets in a period of five years.

The major nationalised industries have organised their investments on the basis of long-term plans. The first of these to appear was the National Coal Board's *Plan for Coal* of 1950. This was succeeded in 1956 by *Investing in Coal*, and in 1959 the *Revised Plan for Coal* was issued. The 1959 Plan envisaged continued reconstruction and development requiring capital expenditure of £11 million between 1960 and 1965. There is a natural tendency in extractive industries for production to get more difficult, and the best and most accessible coal in Britain has already been mined. Investment is therefore needed even to maintain efficiency—for deeper pits and for more mechanisation. The present objective, however, is to increase efficiency and hence to lower costs while maintaining total output. Investment to this end in the early 1960s was running at about £90 million per annum.

The gas industry's first plan, called *Fuel for the Nation*, was published in 1954, and its second, *Gas Looks Ahead*, in 1958. The growth of the industry was on a modest scale in the 1950s. Capital expenditure was divided between new manufacturing plant, inter-connecting pipelines, and distribution of consumers' equipment. Technical progress, more rapid growth of demand, and new sources of supply —notably imported methane —have led to greater develop-ment of the industry in the 1960s, and investment in the next few years is likely to be at £80 million or £90 million per annum.

In 1955 the electricity industry's development plan, *Power and Prosperity*, was issued, and in 1958 their *Power for the Future*. The great increase in demand has meant that investment has had to be very high. In fact, the industry takes about half of all the investment in nationalised industries. New power stations, modernisation of equipment, and the building up of the transmission system are all costly forms of capital expenditure. Annual investment in Great Britain of over £430 million in 1962–3 is expected to rise to £715 million in 1965–6.

The *Modernisation and Re-equipment Plan* for the railways was issued in 1955. This provides for the elimination of steam traction and its replacement by electric and diesel locomotion. Stations, marshalling yards and suburban electrification are also to be improved. The original plan was merged into the scheme for *Re-shaping British Railways* in 1963. Investment in nationalised transport, mostly railways, is now expected to run at about £150 million for the next few years.

Other public investment in the nationalised industries is not on so large a scale. The airlines' needs vary considerably, according to their need for new aircraft. In 1963–4 they amounted to over £34 million. Atomic energy now takes under £30 million a year. Since it is not a public corporation, the Post Office cannot be classed with the other nationalised industries, but it now takes a great deal of public investment, mainly for inland telecommunications: from £126 million in 1962–3 its capital expenditure is expected to rise to £253 million in 1965–6.

For many years it was thought that to vary public investment with the state of the economy was an essential part of full employment and of anti-inflationary policies. During the 1950s, therefore,

FIXED INVESTMENT IN NATIONALISED INDUSTRIES, 1963–4

	£ million	Percentage of national investment
National Coal Board	89·0	1·7
Electricity Council and boards	469·5	9·0
North Scotland H.-E. Board	17·8	0·3
South Scotland Electricity Board	31·5	0·6
Gas Council and boards	92·0	1·8
British Railways Board	95·0	1·8
London Transport Board	18·2	0·3
British Transport Docks Board	4·3	0·1
British Waterways Board	1·6	—
Transport Holding Company	12·8	0·2
British Overseas Airways Corporation	24·0	0·5
British European Airways	10·8	0·2
Total, nationalised industries	866·5	16·6
Fixed investment, public sector★	2,340·0	44·9
Gross fixed investment	5,216·0	100·0

★ Includes Government departments, armed forces, the Post Office, local authorities, and other public corporations.

Source: White Paper on *Loans from the Consolidated Fund 1965–66,* Cmnd. 2624, March 1965.

the nationalised industries were subjected to several cuts, at short
notice, in their capital programmes; at other times they were
encouraged to speed up such work. The resulting dislocation proved
technically damaging and economically expensive. The White
Paper on *Public Investment*[3] of 1960, however, noted that most public
investment was basic to the rest of the economy and that interference
with it, for short-term reasons, could do more harm than good.
In the future, therefore, the improvement of capital in the nationalised industries may proceed more smoothly.

In addition to this change of attitude, there has been improved
information about public investment. There is now an annual White
Paper in the autumn on *Public Investment in Great Britain*, giving an
account of current programmes, and one in the spring on *Loans
from the Consolidated Fund*, explaining how the Government helps to
finance them.

These reforms help to show how investment in nationalised
industries fits in with national economic planning. Since they do not
compete in the market for new capital, the amount of capital to be
provided for each industry has to be determined by other means.
An estimate of the future situation of each industry has to be agreed,
therefore, with the central Government, taking into account the
probable growth of the economy as a whole and the fact that the
various industries are to some extent in competition with one another
and with other suppliers.

In making such calculations, the Government's planning authorities must have some idea of the role they expect nationalised industries to play in the economy and in society. As indicated, the
financial objectives of the industries have been clarified in recent
years, and the success of the corporations in meeting these targets
will presumably help to decide their scale of operations — and hence
their share of national investment in the future. Nevertheless, the
Government has acknowledged the 'public utility' character of
many of the concerns: they are not expected to secure high profits,
and their primary function is to meet the basic economic requirements of the nation. In Chapter 7 this question of the aims of
nationalisation is discussed at length.

Efficiency and technical progress

The object of modernisation and development in industry is to improve the productive process—to make it in some sense more efficient. The investment just described should result in higher productivity and should involve innovation of a technical as well as an organisational nature.

It is not easy to define efficiency, let alone measure it. There is some information about productivity, however, which is relevant.

In the coalmining industry, productivity is usually measured in output per man-shift. At the time of nationalisation, just over one ton per shift was produced for every man in the industry, or 2·9 tons per shift for each worker at the coalface. For a time improvement was slow and in the middle 1950s it came virtually to a standstill—the attempt to secure maximum production meant keeping inefficient high-cost pits in use. But in the 'sixties investment has borne fruit and progress has been rapid—in 1962 nearly 1·6 tons per man-shift was produced, or 4·5 tons per man-shift for faceworkers. This of course does not compare with the situation in the United States, where conditions are much easier, but it is much the same as in Western Europe.

Productivity in the generation of electricity has been aided by technical improvement and by larger generators. In 1948 the thermal efficiency of steam-generating stations was twenty-one per cent; by 1962 it was nearly twenty-eight per cent. In terms of output per employee, productivity has increased considerably—in 1948 a load of 10,263 megawatts was met with 151,000 employees, and for the 1962 load of 32,607 megawatts, only 204,000 employees were necessary. In the gas industry there has been a reduction of half in the number of gas works in operation since nationalisation. The average yield of gas per ton of coal carbonised was seventy-seven therms in 1962, compared with seventy-three therms in 1950. Output per man has risen by five per cent per annum recently. New gas-making processes now promise greater improvements.

The first ten years of nationalisation on the railways brought an increase in efficiency, measured in 'net ton-miles per engine-hour', from 520 to 638: and the average mileage covered per engine without mechanical failure doubled. The British Railways Productivity Council was established in May 1955 to promote work-study schemes in all branches of railway operation, but the progress of its work has not been rapid.

Ways of measuring the efficiency of airlines include the relation of the 'capacity' of the line, measured in ton-miles, to the number of employees. This has increased fourfold since nationalisation in B.O.A.C. and fivefold in B.E.A. Some elaborate comparisons with foreign airlines were attempted in 1959.[4]

These measures of productivity are not the only possible ones, and there is room for argument about their value as tests of efficiency. Some improvement is to be expected from investment and technical progress; the question is whether the degree of improvement reflects adequately the resources that have been put in. For this reason the return on capital that is being used offers a more general measure of the efficiency of the industries, and this is usually the form in which the Government's financial objectives for them have been cast. Again, the place of this type of objective among the aims of nationalisation is further considered in Chapter 7.

Improvement in efficiency does not happen merely by pouring in money. It is dependent in the long run on technical innovation, and this in turn is sustained by research. All the major nationalised industries have research programmes and research organisations.

In the National Coal Board there are three main avenues of research. The Mining Research Establishment, at Isleworth in Middlesex, is concerned with the actual process of mining — coal-getting techniques, tunnelling, safety, and so on. The Coal Research Establishment at Stoke Orchard, near Cheltenham, deals with the fuel itself and its by-products; it was particularly concerned with the development of the smokeless fuel, 'Homefire'. At Bretby there is a Central Engineering Establishment, which develops machinery for use in the industry. The Coal Board does not itself manufacture machinery, and the Establishment therefore works in collaboration with the manufacturers. There are also numbers of other research activities connected with the industry, including the Coal Survey (absorbed in the Board's general scientific organisation in 1961), which explores the country's reserves of coal and helps to plan their exploitation.

Similarly, the other nationalised corporations have central research institutions (the Central Electricity Research Laboratories at Leatherhead, the research stations of the Gas Council in London and Solihull, the Cavendish House Laboratories of British Railways at Derby); and they sponsor other research projects, either at smaller stations or attached to the operations of the industry. In addition, nationalised industries are important supporters of research associations—the Coal Utilisation Research Association and the British Electrical and Allied Industries Research Association, for example. They may also be interested in (and subscribe to) the work of bodies such as the Medical Research Council, and they finance particular research projects in the universities.

It is impossible to assess by means of a general survey the effectiveness of research. It is of the greatest importance that the investigations should be related to the actual problems of the industry; it is equally vital that management should have the scientific understanding necessary to grasp the significance of what has been done and what could be done. Only with this mutual comprehension will research be seen as part of the essential progress of the industries, and not merely as a marginal good cause. The promotion of research is thus only partly a matter of finance and manpower: it also depends on good organisation and communication.

The research position in British industry was considered to be generally weak in the 1950s and has since been strengthened. It was heavily concentrated in the aircraft-construction and electrical industries. The nationalised industries reflect these variations. The airlines rely largely on other bodies—the constructors and the Aeronautical Research Council. The Coal Board has built up its activities from scratch; others have had to expand existing arrangements as well as they could. A difficulty for some—coal, gas, the railways—has been the unglamorous image of their industry: they were unable to attract brilliant minds in the way that electronics and atomic energy could. An increase in scientific manpower and greater awareness of the value of technology compared with pure science may help to ease the situation.

The Atomic Energy Authority, of course, has not been faced with the same sort of problem. It is the most striking example of a 'science-based' industry, where the problem is to build effective production out of creative discovery, rather than to apply scientific research to established and often conservative industries.

In practical terms, the years of nationalisation have brought great technical changes to the industries. Sixty per cent of coal is power-loaded, and coal-cutting machinery has become almost universal. The average size of power stations has risen from under 50 megawatts on nationalisation to 130 megawatts in the 1960s, and some stations of 400, 500, and even 600 megawatts' capacity were in operation by 1962. New gasification processes, the use of methane, and better domestic appliances are transforming the uses of gas. Steam is being replaced by electrical and diesel traction on the railways. Airlines now fly jet liners, whereas routes once had to be pioneered with converted troop transports. Such rapid changes are characteristic of twentieth-century civilisation: they provide the material with which systems of management must cope. The critical question for efficiency is whether nationalisation can provide a style of organisation that enhances development rather than retards it.

Labour relations

For many advocates of public ownership the improvement — indeed, the transformation — of labour relations was the main object of the change. Under capitalism, it was thought, workers could not be treated fairly, because all other interests had to be sacrificed to the need to make as much profit as possible. A publicly owned enterprise would be under no such compulsion and therefore could be expected to treat its employees honestly and decently. When this became recognised, the bitterness would disappear from industrial negotiations and an atmosphere of understanding, and eventually of co-operation, would be achieved. These expectations were strongest, of course, among those for whom socialism was a moral crusade: if the causes of social injustice were removed, then greater harmony might reasonably be hoped for.

The form chosen to implement public ownership was, however, the managerial public corporation. No fundamental change was made in the status of the workers, who remained employees with no direct voice in the control of their enterprises. The Acts merely made negotiating machinery and joint consultation compulsory.

The trade unions remained independent and necessary organisations, bargaining with employers about wages and conditions as before. In these circumstances the improvement of labour relations became a matter of patient, step-by-step amelioration, of the gradual breaking down of traditional attitudes. Progress was slow and halting, constantly bedevilled by economic stringencies and social frustrations.

Events in this field have caused disappointment in some quarters and allegations of failure from others. The truth is that much disillusion was inevitable because hopes were pitched far too high, and because they rested on a mistaken diagnosis of the causes of industrial conflict. Moreover, there are strong political arguments for the trade unions' maintaining an independent position and not taking any share in or responsibility for management decisions. For if they do become so involved, the workers will find themselves once again individuals and subordinates in a hierarchical system, without the protection for their rights or influence for their desires which independent collective organisation brings.[5]

Though nationalisation cannot claim to be the solution to industrial conflict, the principle it embodies does have some relevance to the problem. Public corporations have an explicit responsibility to the nation, enforced by a deliberate system of accountability and control. Their policies are therefore tied to public opinion—at any rate, in so far as this is manifested through the machinery of political democracy. And if this conception involves the provision of services, or the setting of prices, or the acceptance of fair standards that might appear uneconomic or unnecessary to a private business, then the public corporation must acknowledge its wider responsibilities. 'Having willed the end, the Nation must will the means,' said a court of inquiry in a wage dispute.[6] In other words, labour relations in nationalised industries are affected by the fact that public employers have a duty to serve the national interest, not vaguely and indirectly, but in a precise way that can be determined by the Government.

Nation-wide official strikes have become uncommon in Britain since the arrival of full employment. In publicly owned as in private industry, most strikes have occurred in particular places, over local disputes, and have often been unofficial.

There have been exceptions. On the railways the Amalgamated Society of Locomotive Engineers and Firemen struck over pay differentials for seventeen days in 1955. The London busmen struck for forty-seven days in 1958. The National Union of Railwaymen held a one-day token strike on October 3rd, 1962. Moreover, partial strikes and unofficial stoppages and go-slows can have considerable impact, not only as industrial weapons, but also on public opinion. The record of nationalised industries has not been so strike-free as to demonstrate any obvious superiority of public enterprise in this respect.

The coal industry presents the most paradoxical situation. On the one hand, there have been no national strikes since nationalisation. Yet the industry is the most strike-prone in the country, and a high proportion of all the industrial disputes recorded by the Ministry of Labour occur in the mines. The causes are to be found in the organisation and traditions of the miners' working lives, rather than in comparative economic circumstances. Their effect on total production is small, for usually less than one per cent of national output per year is lost.

Nationalisation has given further impetus to the tendency to centralise wage bargaining. In nationalised industries the main wage and salary settlements are made between the boards and large unions, and are negotiated at national level. National wage agreements, at least on basic scales, are insisted on by most trade unions, and they embody the belief that people doing the same work should get the same pay. But the creation of national public corporations as employers has increased the unions' determination to present a strong and, if possible, united front in negotiation with them. There may be deeper social forces at work in some cases: for example, decentralisation of the coal industry is resisted by the National Union of Mineworkers in case it should 'set coalfield against coalfield'. They fear that miners with lower wages in one field might be helping to undercut the sales and hence the prosperity of another coalfield.

The most controversial aspect of wage negotiations in nationalised industries has been the part played by the Government. (This is discussed as a form of ministerial control in Chapter 6.) It has sometimes been alleged that in the 1950s publicly owned industries took the lead in granting wage increases to their employees, and that this initiated inflationary wage rounds throughout industry. In retrospect, however, there seems little evidence that nationalised industries were often in the lead with concessions. On the contrary, many of the critical disputes — on the railways, for example — arose because wage standards had fallen behind those in other occupations. The truth of the matter seems to be that certain occupations apparently take the lead in raising wage rates, but these are in industries where there is little or no payment above the standard rates. Raising wage rates in these occupations is often necessary to catch up with *earnings* that have already risen above standard rates elsewhere. Such occupations include work in electricity supply and on the London buses, but they also include private employments like multiple grocery stores and agriculture.

Over the years since nationalisation was established, wage rates in nationalised industries have more or less kept pace with those elsewhere: in gas and electricity they have risen a little more than average; in road haulage, London buses, and on the canals rather less.[7] Besides wages, other benefits such as sick pay and pensions have improved, and there are redundancy schemes in all nationalised industries.

In two directions, however, the nationalised industries can claim to have made considerable improvements in labour matters. First, they have developed training programmes and promotion schemes. Second, they have given much attention to the processes of joint consultation.

Every major nationalised industry has set up a scheme whereby workers in the industry can progress, by internal training and experience, to better jobs and to higher levels of skill and authority. One of the best known is the 'ladder plan' of the National Coal Board. This provides a series of schemes for young men entering the industry, by which they can become tradesmen, deputies, or technicians, or they can enter managerial grades. Day-release and even full-time courses are made available to assist the progress of employees. The N.C.B. also has management-development schemes—providing university scholarships, directed practical training, and experience for non-technical administrators. The other public corporations have similar schemes, adapted to their own structures and requirements.

The boards have a statutory obligation to submit education and training plans to the appropriate Minister for his approval, and this may have compelled them to give special attention to the matter. But in fact, the position of the boards as managers of whole industries gives them both the incentive and the ability to develop technical and managerial skills. To do so is just as important for their future as to invest in new capital. Their resources and influence enable them to make sure that the necessary facilities are available. Moreover, it is clearly their business to do so, for they cannot hope to recruit people to their specific requirements from anywhere else. Large organisations are in general well placed to offer varied and extensive career opportunities, and it is vital for morale that the nationalised industries should exploit this advantage to the full.

The concept of the managerial public corporation debars employees and their unions from any direct responsibility for running the industries. Nevertheless, machinery for regular consultation between management at all levels and organised labour has been set up. This does not detract from the powers of management to take decisions; but it is designed to ensure that both sides are aware of the facts, and of the views and motives of each other. Where it works effectively, joint consultation makes an outstanding contribution to mutual understanding and to the problem of industrial 'communications'.[8]

There are difficulties, however, in many cases. Foremen and supervisors are apt to resent being bypassed when workers on consultative committees have access to higher levels of management than they do. Some managers regard the system as an unpleasant duty to be carried through as quickly as possible. Workers' representatives sometimes show little interest in matters beyond their immediate conditions of employment. In short, joint consultation cannot be made effective by mere establishment of the machinery of committees. It requires patience and, in view of the wide scope of potential subject matter, a great amount of study and thought by all participants.

Some advocates of nationalisation hoped that, if it did not change the form of labour relations, it would at least create a new professional spirit among its administrators and imbue its workers with the idea of public service.[9] A new type of manager, who would combine the high responsibility and dedication of the civil servant with the drive and initiative of the businessman, was foreseen. Since these changes were not expected overnight but might take a generation to emerge, it is still premature to assess results. The training schemes and plans for management development should help progress in this direction. Yet in matters of morale and social values the influence of leadership is all-important. Conservative ministers have accepted nationalisation, but they have not felt able to extol its virtues. Nor have Board members (with some exceptions, usually at the Coal Board) gone out of their way to emphasise the merits of public enterprise as such —no doubt some of them, being ex-businessmen, have doubted the existence of merits. In these circumstances pride in achievement and in technical progress is possible; but while the need to emulate business success is stressed at the top, it is not likely that any very distinctive outlook will flourish in the service of the corporations.

As stated at the outset of this chapter, the record of the nationalised industries does not enable judgments to be made about their success. There has been undoubted progress and achievement: but how can their adequacy be reckoned? There have been weaknesses and commercial troubles: are the explanations of these satisfactory?

In sum, the financial record of nationalised industries has been chequered, with several corporations making serious losses, and one, the railways, being in deep, long-run trouble. These losses have been the chief target of nationalisation's critics, and accounting for them is a field of complex argument. The investment programmes have been large—some critics in the past suggested over-large. The industries have shown much energy in pursuing technical progress, so far as capital has been available. Beyond this, questions of commercial policy and harmonisation with the national interest have complicated the simple issues of efficiency and profitability. Labour relations have improved, but whether they are what they could be is much disputed. In brief, the facts about nationalisation in practice only lead to further problems and controversies. Many of these are discussed in the following chapters.

5 Problems of Organisation

Controversy about nationalisation, even heated controversy, has not been confined to the principle itself. The methods, supervision, and objectives of the nationalised industries have been subjected to vigorous criticism.

In this chapter and the two that follow, some of the main areas of controversy will be explored. So far this book has been concerned with the facts, historical and structural, of nationalisation as it exists. It will continue to set out the essentials of what has been done, but more and more it will be necessary to consider views expressed about these actions, and to try to form an assessment of their merits.

The first set of problems to be examined are organisational. These are practical matters, on which the lines of dispute are not often partisan in the political sense — although the opinions expressed are not less vehement for that reason.

The principle of nationalisation, as distinct from municipalisation or selective public ownership, has carried with it the notion of unification on a country-wide scale. Usually a single general organisation has been set up for each industry. Since the industries are major ones, the size of each organisation tends to be very large.

Two of the nationalised undertakings, coalmining and the railways, are much larger than any other industrial enterprise in Britain. The National Coal Board employed about 605,000 people in 1963, and British Railways 460,000. At its peak, in the early 1950s, the British Transport Commission had nearly 1,000,000 employees. The other main industries are smaller than these, but still of considerable magnitude by any industrial standard. The electricity industry had 210,000 employees in 1963 and gas employed 123,000. Large operational units included the Central Electricity

Generating Board, with 61,000; the London Electricity Board with 16,000, and the North Thames Gas Board with 22,000 employees. Besides railways in transport were London Transport with 74,000 on its payroll, and British Road Services, employing 35,000 people.

Measured by employment, the airlines are among the lesser of the nationalised industries. Yet in 1963 the British Overseas Airways Corporation employed 21,000 people, and British European Airways 17,000. These sizes may be compared with those of other industrial units. The Post Office employs about 350,000 people. Imperial Chemical Industries Ltd, one of the largest private-enterprise concerns in the country, has 160,000 people in its employment. Unilever, a multi-product firm with interests in many countries, employs about 300,000 people altogether. The world-wide employment of General Motors and its subsidiaries was 660,000 in 1964.

Two channels of intellectual inquiry were available for examining the problems of organisation in nationalised industries—the study of public administration and that of industrial management. These had traditionally kept apart, and it cannot be said that anything approaching unification has been achieved in face of common problems. Clearly each approach has valuable contributions to make. In the study of public administration some understanding of the concepts of responsibility, accountability, and political policy-making had been achieved by 1945; from industrial management, ideas about the authority of boards, decentralisation, and standard tests of performance were obtained.

It was generally agreed that the process of take-over and transition to public ownership was smoothly and efficiently accomplished, in spite of many difficulties. But serious organisational issues soon arose, and some account of them must now be given.

GOVERNING BOARDS

It is implicit in the concept of the public corporation that there should be a board or council of some sort in charge of affairs. Within the organisation this body has full authority, and its composition is clearly crucial for the success of the whole enterprise.

The rejection of the representative board has been described in Chapter 2. The Port of London Authority had such a board, but the public corporations set up between the wars consisted of independent managers without outside connections or responsibilities. In the case of the London Passenger Transport Board, members were appointed by a special group of appointing trustees indicated in the statute.[1] But in other cases appointment by the Minister was the rule; and even where the Crown made the appointments, it was in fact done on the advice of the Government. In short, the board all derived their positions from the same source and were expected to work as a team.

The post-war public corporations are very similar to one another in their practices concerning the governing boards, partly as a result of earlier experience, and partly because they were all constituted within a few years of each other by the same Government. It is therefore possible to consider a body of standard practices, with only a few variations, and criticisms of these practices.

The name of the governing board varies—Board, Commission, Council, Authority—but these differences appear to have no practical consequences. There is also some variation in the size of the boards, upper and lower limits being fixed by each statute. Among the largest are the Electricity Council and the Gas Council, with twenty and fourteen members respectively, but both these consist largely of the chairmen of Area Boards. The Central Electricity Generating Board has nine members, the National Coal Board has eleven, and the British Railways Board fifteen, and this appears to be the usual range for effective working.

The main standard practices may now be indicated. The first, as stated, is appointment by the Minister or the Crown on the advice of the Government. This at once shows the political foundations of the boards' authority, and provides a major means of governmental control. The chairmen and deputy-chairmen are designated as such —that is to say, they are chosen by the Minister and not by their fellow-members on the boards.

Secondly, there are some statutory qualifications for membership. Normally these are very wide. The Minister may appoint to the

National Coal Board 'persons appearing to him to be qualified as having had experience of, and having shown capacity in, industrial, commercial or financial matters, applied science, administration or the organisation of workers'.

With some modifications, formulae like this are applied to the other nationalised industries. The phrase 'organisation of workers' emphasises the right of trade unionists as such to serve on the boards. There are also some disqualifications: membership of the House of Commons, engaging in trade or business, or becoming of unsound mind are frequent bars to continuing service. Membership of the House of Lords is not a disqualification, and in fact several notable leaders of the industries have been peers. Nor are there any specific political qualifications or disqualifications. Lord Robens was a member of the Opposition front bench when appointed, by the Conservative Government, to the National Coal Board, and other persons with well-known Conservative or Labour sympathies have served on the boards.

Thirdly, there are no formal nominations for places on the boards. Unions, stockholders, or customers have no right to have particular persons put on the boards. Nevertheless, it is prudent and desirable for a minister to take soundings before making appointments. These no doubt include civil servants in the Ministry, Government and Party colleagues, trade unions, and perhaps existing members of the boards, including part-time members. All these consultations are private, however, and do not bind a minister, though he would scarcely make an important appointment without the concurrence of the Prime Minister.

Fourthly, appointments are made for a limited period, most commonly five years. These may be renewed, and appointments are staggered so that whole boards are not changed at the same time. Board membership is not necessarily affected by changes of government, even when there is a change of party control. Members of boards may of course resign at any time; and, more significantly, they may be dismissed by the Minister. This he may do for reasons of alleged incapacity, neglect, or inefficiency; and it is clear that he can at least force resignation in cases of severe policy disagreement.

Fifthly, the rules about qualifications and consultation make it possible for members to come from outside the industries concerned. In fact, most of the appointments are promotions of successful managers from inside the corporations; but there continues to be a significant group who did not rise in this way. For example, Lord Robens, Dr Richard Beeching, and Sir Ronald Edwards — holding probably the three senior positions in the nationalised industries in 1964 — were all brought in from other employment. Furthermore, the practice of appointing trade unionists has not meant that the individuals concerned were from the unions in the industry. Thus in 1964 the Railways Board had Mr Hayday from the General and Municipal Workers' Union, and the Coal Board had Mr Webber, who had been an official of the union for transport salaried staff.

It is now the custom to appoint some part-time members to the boards. Sometimes these constitute a majority. The British Transport Docks Board and the British Waterways Board each has only one full-time member, the chairman; all the rest serve part time. On the Coal Board, the Railways Board, and the Electricity Generating Board, however, there is a comparatively small group of part-timers supplementing a majority of full-time members. The function of this latter type of member is to bring wider experience into the industries, to provide knowledge of practices of other bodies for comparative purposes, and to give regular contact with people who are not constantly occupied with the details of the industry. It is hoped, that is to say, that this element in the boards will help them to see the wood as well as the trees.

Some criticisms of these standard practices may now be considered.

It has been suggested by left-wing critics that the result of the system has been a preponderance of businessmen on the boards, and that these may be assumed to be hostile to nationalisation in principle and unenthusiastic about it in particular cases. Mr Clive Jenkins has shown that, in 1956, out of 272 members of boards of public corporations (including Area Boards), 106 were also directors of private-enterprise concerns.[2]

Most of these appointments are of part-time members, however, and the influence of such members rarely predominates whatever their numerical strength. Moreover, in a community where most of industry is privately owned, it is natural that the greatest supply of managerial talent is to be found there. If outside people are to be brought in (and where industries are being reconstructed the case for doing so is overwhelming), then many must come from private enterprise. This is not to say that morale and confidence in nationalisation are irrelevant, but that they depend on political encouragement and a few key appointments rather than numerical balance.

At one time there was also criticism of the amateurism of the boards, and of the appointment of 'retired generals, admirals, etc.' Much of this was misconceived, for the soldiers and sailors were service engineers, transport experts, and so on; and in the post-war period there was a supply of ex-service talent available which it would have been pointless to neglect. The practice of making such appointments, and hence the criticism, seems to have diminished in recent years.

It will be convenient in assessing the composition of the boards to consider possible alternatives. A radical revision of the practices that had grown up was proposed by Lord Simon of Wythenshawe in 1957.[3] Lord Simon contrasted practices in public corporations with those of large private firms, particularly Imperial Chemical Industries Ltd. He argued that board members should normally be appointed from within the industry, on the recommendation of the existing board, and should serve until retirement. To this end, management-development programmes in the industries should be improved, and should lead up to the boards themselves. Ministerial control and accountability to Parliament should not interfere with the effective power of the board.

This plan would change radically the position of the boards, by increasing their security and independent authority. In spirit it involves a reversion to pre-war practice, when there was minimal political control. The ability of Ministers to assert their authority — although legally present — would become in practice very difficult. In fact, there is wide assent to most of Lord Simon's sentiments, certainly to the proposition that eventually board members should be recruited from within the corporations. But even this is not regarded as applicable in a rigid way, and at present the need for rehabilitation of some industries is held to emphasise the need to bring in proved talent with new ideas from outside. In any case, whatever may become normal practice, the right of the Minister to apply or vary the practice is a crucial political responsibility which is unlikely to be forgone.

The question of security of tenure for board members up to retiring age is more controversial.[4] Again, Ministers are willing in most cases to reappoint ordinary board members for successive terms. But there is no guarantee that this will happen, and a board member —particularly a chairman—must feel that disagreement with ministerial ideas will reduce the chance of his continuance in office. The prospect of this insecurity may deter some from accepting board posts. The issue is fundamentally one of the degree of independence that a public corporation can enjoy: whether it may expect to develop a general outlook of its own, or whether it should take its broad philosophy from the elected Government. (This question is the theme of Chapter 6.) However, the possibility of a Government's allowing independence depends in turn on public opinion; if blame is ascribed to Ministers for the state of an industry, then they may be expected to exert maximum powers of control, in order to satisfy themselves that things are going as well as they can make them.

The question of the proper salaries for board members has been one of great difficulty. It arises primarily because of the double aspect of the corporations, as both public services and industrial concerns—and from the fact that there is customarily considerable disparity of payment between these activities.

The general run of salaries (revised in April 1964) for the boards of nationalised industries is as follows:

Main boards	per annum
Chairman	£11,000 to £12,500
Deputy-chairman	£7,500 to £10,000
Member	£7,000 to £9,500

Area boards	*per annum*
Chairman	£7,000 to £9,500
Deputy-chairman	£5,500 to £6,500
Member	£4,500 to £5,500

These salaries are for full-time members; for part-time members a payment of £1,000 a year is customary. There have been exceptions to the above rates, the principal ones concerning the British Railways Board, where the chairman from 1961 to 1965, Dr Richard Beeching, was paid £24,000 a year and one full-time member £12,000. Sir Giles Guthrie, chairman and managing director of B.O.A.C. since January 1964, has £15,000 a year.

Many critics, including Lord Simon, have held that the salaries (and allowances, pensions, etc.) should be at least as great as those in leading private-enterprise firms. The Labour Party, in a pamphlet issued in 1957, stated that 'the salaries paid should not be markedly less than those for similar jobs in private business.'[5]

They are clearly not of this order at present. The grounds for paying Dr Beeching £24,000 were that this amount was paid to him as an ordinary director of I.C.I. Ltd. Moreover, the accounts of other companies show very large sums paid to their boards of directors, so that each member must get more than the standard indicated for public boards. Of course, tax deductions are considerable at this level. Nevertheless, there is a contrast between business and public-service payments—even after the changes of November 1964, the Prime Minister is paid £14,000 per annum, ordinary departmental ministers £8,500, the chief civil servant of a department £6,950, and Members of Parliament £3,250.

There are thus two main arguments for high salaries—possibly higher than at present—for members of the boards of public corporations. The first is the need to keep and sometimes to recruit high-quality people, in the face of the attractions of private industry. The second is the need for adequate differentials between management levels, so that promotion brings appreciable material rewards—and board salaries determine the ceiling under which other scales must be arranged. On the other hand, there is no case for paying more than is reasonable in the circumstances, or for chasing what many consider to be inflated and socially undesirable levels of remuneration, if it can be avoided. The ideas of public service and of national status may have some influence: judges, at £8,000 a year, are paid less than many successful barristers. Nevertheless, it is not at present practicable, in a mixed economy, to use the public corporations to set the standards for the general range of remuneration in society; and this being so, substantial salaries, influenced by competition from private industry, must be paid for high industrial posts.

The role of the boards

Though all public corporations must have a board of some sort at the head of their affairs, the purpose of this body and the manner in which it exercises its powers have been the subject of extensive dispute.

The controversy lies mainly between supporters of the *functional board*, sometimes called the executive or managerial board, and those who advocate the *policy board*, or one with mainly supervisory duties. The functional board takes direct control of the affairs of the corporation, each member (apart from the chairman and perhaps deputy-chairman) exercising control over a particular aspect of the industry, through a department of the headquarters' organisation. In the policy board the members have only general responsibilities, and the actual running of the industry is carried on by senior executives appointed by the board. Thus the board discusses and determines the policy to be pursued in any field of activity, but it leaves its execution to others.

The most striking example of the supervisory board comes from a public corporation outside the main industrial complex, the British Broadcasting Corporation. This has a board of governors of seven part-time members, whose duties are broadly supervisory. In fact the B.B.C. has always been run by its Director-General, in whom full executive authority is vested, including control over programmes. This distribution of power was established in the time of Lord Reith, the first Director-General, a man of strong will and

determination, and has been little modified since. In this case it
seems that the Director-General must not only exercise administrative power, but must also have great influence on policy. When
the post-war corporations were set up, most national boards had a
functional or executive nature, though the Gas Council and the
original British Transport Commission were mainly concerned with
co-ordination.

The arguments for the functional board turn on the need for
realism and effective authority. Only if board members are in day-
to-day touch with problems and if they must personally carry out
what has to be done, it is said, will they fully appreciate the necessities of a situation. If they can proceed by passing orders to others,
they will become remote and perhaps perfectionist; and they may
develop ideas at variance with those of their senior executives,
causing disharmony and inefficiency. The functional board fixes
responsibility: the members themselves decide what is to be done
and do it, and there is no room for misunderstanding or shifting the
blame.

For the policy board it is said that it gives its members time to
think about major policy and to reflect on future development.
They do not become absorbed in detail, and they can stand aloof
from disagreements and minor problems. They can, moreover, be
mindful of the corporation's responsibilities to the public and its
attitude to Government policy. This system permits devolution of
responsibility and thus gives scope for initiative and decentralised
authority.

The views of the Fleck and Herbert committees were at variance
on this as on other matters. The Fleck report provided for each
board member's having specific responsibilities, and it recommended
that 'the board should insist on their policies being properly carried
out by the subordinate formations and should ensure that discipline
obtains'. The Herbert committee, on the other hand, saw the board
as 'a group of men ... ready to help, to co-ordinate and to stimulate,
and relying on direction only where persuasion fails'.[6]

In the industrial public corporations, variations in arrangements
continue, though some similarities have emerged. The Electricity

Council is clearly a policy board, but then it is stronger than the B.B.C. governors, and those members drawn from Area Electricity Boards have functional responsibilities. In other boards the usual practice is for the board to regard itself primarily as a policy board, but for the full-time members to take a particular interest in one or more aspects of the corporation's work, and to work closely with the headquarters' executives in these fields. The chairman, deputy-chairman, and part-time members ensure that a board's business is centred on major issues, and that it does not become so preoccupied with internal harmony as to neglect its wider responsibilities.

These arrangements seem to be working fairly well in most cases. It is possible that the need for a functional board or a policy board varies not only with the structure of the various industries, but also from time to time in each industry as its main problems change. One factor that must be borne in mind is the position of the Minister. If he and his department, wisely or unwisely, exercise a close supervisory interest, or if the Government has itself prescribed particular policies for an industry, then the need for a policy board declines. This raises, of course, the problem of ministerial control discussed in Chapter 6.

In any case, the proper role of the board depends to some extent on the nature of the structure beneath it. The degree of centralisation and decentralisation in nationalised organisations must therefore be discussed.

CENTRALISATION AND DECENTRALISATION

The main practical problem of organisation for a public corporation lies in the extent to which its operations shall be controlled by central authority, or shall be devolved to lesser bodies. This is regularly a matter of hot contention, on which there is not infrequently more than a whiff of dogma on either side.

For each corporation the basic situation is prescribed by statute. As explained in Chapter 3, the original statutes tended to give more detail, and to impose more decentralisation, as the process of nationalisation progressed between 1946 and 1949. By statute, therefore, the National Coal Board is not decentralised, and the Gas Council is; and the nationalised steel industry between 1950 and 1953 had, in the existing firms, even more devolved authorities.

A distinction may be drawn between geographical and functional decentralisation. In many corporations there are subordinate authorities in different parts of the country —divisions, areas, or regions. There is also separation, however, between different processes and stages of production —in electricity, for example, between generation and distribution.

Although no subordinate formations were prescribed in the Nationalisation Act of 1946, the National Coal Board set up a structure which broadly survived until the end of 1965. There were nine Divisions in the main coalfields, each of which controlled a number of Areas. The Areas became the main operational units of the industry, each running many pits. The Divisions had a divisional board in control, appointed by the National Coal Board. Areas were controlled by area general managers (called Directors after 1965), always appointed by the national board, not the divisional one. Before 1965 there were usually Groups within the Areas. The collieries themselves are controlled by managers, who are mining engineers. This is essentially a production organisation; there is in addition a system of Regions, concerned with general distribution and covering the whole country, not merely the coalfields.

In the original Acts both the electricity and gas industries were provided with Area organisations, controlled by boards appointed by the Minister himself. In electricity these are concerned with distribution to the consumer; in gas they are responsible for both manufacture and distribution. The original British Electricity Authority of 1947 was both a generating and a supervisory body; and the Area Boards were represented on it by four of their number in rotation. The Gas Council is largely a federal body: apart from chairman and deputy-chairman, it consists entirely of the chairmen of Area Boards. Thus, in contrast to some of the other industries, the main focus of operations in gas and electricity distribution is the Area: the national bodies have co-ordinating and general-policy functions.

The British Transport Commission of 1947 was a co-ordinating body over a number of functional Executives. Some of these had their own schemes of devolution, and to some extent a regional system persisted in the railways, based largely on the old main-line companies. The two nationalised airlines have no subsidiary authorities, though considerable autonomy must be given to officials operating abroad.

The arguments about decentralisation that took place in the 1950s must now be examined. They were particularly concerned with the coal and electricity industries, though in fact important developments in the administration of the railways have also taken place.

The creation of the National Coal Board as a large unified organisation was a complete transformation for the coal industry, which had previously consisted, in the main, of relatively small firms. The new structure was soon subjected to attack. The early resignation from the Coal Board of Sir Charles Reid was followed by articles in *The Times* in which he set out a new structure for the industry, abolishing Divisions and giving great autonomy to twenty-six 'corporations'. Further criticisms followed, notably from Conservative Party sources.[7] The N.C.B. therefore asked one of its members, Sir Robert Burrows, to conduct an inquiry into the organisation of the industry.

Sir Robert's report was made in 1948 and is summarised in the Coal Board's annual report for that year.[8] Besides changes in the constitution of the national board, it suggested further decentralising moves — executive power should pass from Divisions to Areas, and the position of colliery managers should be strengthened. The national board should leave executive action to its officials. Some proposals of the Burrows report were put into effect with the aid of the Coal Industry Act, 1949.

Demands for the radical decentralisation of various nationalised industries continued. The Acton Society Trust in 1951 produced reports on the *Extent of Decentralisation* and *Patterns of Organisation*, criticising the size and centralisation of the corporations. The most drastic plans were set out in 1953 by Professor T. E. Chester and Mr Hugh Clegg in *The Future of Nationalisation*. This book condemned the creation of unified national bodies to run whole industries, since this almost inevitably led to over-centralisation. In the first place, the very existence of a central authority with full powers meant that grievances and disputes were normally pursued to that level, and the taking of most decisions at headquarters became habitual. Secondly, it made a hierarchy of control necessary, and in a large organisation this meant a tall 'pyramid' with inevitable remoteness at the top. They recommended that the actual ownership should be held by production units more of the size of large firms, while over them regional and national organisations with functions limited by statute would meet the need for some general co-ordination. Chester and Clegg described how such a structure might be devised, not only for coal, but for the other nationalised concerns as well.

The National Coal Board continued with its basic structure unaltered, but it was influenced by the general climate favouring decentralisation. In October 1953 the board issued a general directive on organisation which stated, among other things, that 'Divisional Boards are bound to consider but not necessarily to accept the advice or suggestions of Headquarters' Departments', and in general it emphasised that various levels of authority had advisory or service functions in relation to one another. Shortly after the circulation of this directive, the N.C.B. appointed a special committee of outside experts to carry out a full review of its organisation. The committee, under the leadership of Dr Alexander Fleck, the chairman of Imperial Chemical Industries Ltd, reported in February 1955.[9] It reversed the whole trend of criticism and development of the previous eight years, and its assessment is worthy of careful examination. Among its findings were:

(a) The basic structure of the board's organisation was sound and should not be altered. It was correctly based on the principle of 'line and staff'. This means that there is a direct line of command from national board to coalface, and that the authorities on it (divisional board, area general manager, colliery manager, etc.) have the power and the duty to impose broad policy. To each level is attached specialist staff, and these communicate with corresponding specialists by 'functional' channels without necessarily involving 'line' authorities. Nevertheless, the committee insisted that the views of specialists at superior levels should normally prevail, and should not be considered merely advisory.

(b) The N.C.B. had mistaken the meaning of decentralisation. 'The board appear to have assumed that decentralisation means that they should not, or need not, impose their will on Divisions and Areas. We do not agree with this policy.' Properly understood, decentralisation means that each level specifies the powers to be exercised by the level below, and leaves it free to exercise them; it does not mean that superior-level policies can be ignored.

(c) Control should be exercised, not by interference, but by modern techniques of approved programmes, periodical reviews, and inspections. It was right for the board's headquarters to scrutinise major capital projects very carefully, and the right of area general managers to authorise projects should be reduced from £100,000 to £50,000. Attention should be given to devising adequate performance standards for collieries, as distinct from forecasts. A scheme for control of operational expenditure by standard costs should be imposed without delay.

(d) Divisions should be retained, and divisional headquarters organised on a common pattern. Areas should also continue, the area general manager in control to have an assistant. The manager need not be a mining engineer.

(e) Colliery managers, who had 'been taught to mine but not how to manage', should have assistance and attend special training courses.

(f) The general directive of October 1953 should be withdrawn and replaced by a more forceful document.

The Fleck report ended the period of hesitant decentralisation in the National Coal Board, and most of its recommendations were carried out swiftly and effectively under a new chairman, Sir James Bowman. A new general directive was issued in July 1955.

In the electricity industry, events took a very different turn in the mid-1950s. The Government appointed a committee under the chairmanship of Sir Edwin Herbert 'to inquire into the organisation and efficiency of the electricity supply industry'. From these wide terms of reference a number of important conclusions emerged. The principal ones concerning organisation were:

(a) The separation of generation from distribution was sound, but there should be a further separation of generation from general supervision and policy-making. A new generating board should therefore be set up.

(b) More freedom should be given to Area Boards in a number of respects, and in general control should be 'judicious and stimulating'. The headquarters staff of the corporation was too large, and both the Area Boards and subordinate officials on the generating side complained of too much interference. This led to confusion of responsibility, and overoccupation with detail at the top.

(c) The central headquarters took too long to approve and took too close an interest in the design and planning of generating stations.

(d) Area Boards should allow district managers to run their own shows and to exercise discretion in dealing with labour and the public.

The Government accepted the main principles of these recommendations, and by the Electricity Act of 1957 a new structure broadly in line with the proposals was set up. Sir Ronald Edwards (a member of the Herbert committee) eventually became chairman of the new supervisory Electricity Council.

There is a clear contrast of general philosophy on organisational matters between the Fleck and Herbert reports, and almost direct

contradiction on particular topics. To some extent this may be due
to differences between the industries, and differences between the
condition of the industries at the time. It is clear, however, that
when lower-level officials complained to the Herbert committee of
frustration, they were listened to sympathetically. The Fleck
committee was less well disposed to these complaints, and perhaps
judged harshly the quality of these personnel. They thought that
it was prudent in the circumstances for higher-level (and more
capable) officials to be able to impose their expertise. Again this may
reflect genuine differences: the shortage of specialist skills in the
coal industry meant that talent was most economically used if
located with relatively high-level authorities.

It is now many years since the Fleck and Herbert reports were
published, and the organisational problems of the industries are not
what they were. In coal, several developments present a need for
organisational change—the physical concentration of the industry
into fewer and larger pits; the growing number of qualified men;
the completion of the building up of strong central services, and the
growth of competition from other fuels. There has been some
cautious functional decentralisation, and independent executives for
brickmaking, coal products, and opencast working have been set up.
In December 1965 a more drastic reorganisation was announced,
to be carried out between 1966 and 1970. Divisions and Groups
were to be eliminated, and Areas reduced in number. The main
problem for the N.C.B., however, is to devise adequate techniques
of accountability for their Areas, so that, with checks on their
efficiency, they can be given greater autonomy. There has also been
some decentralisation in electricity generation, with project groups
and regions now responsible for most operations. The Fleck and
Herbert reports seem destined to become classics of their kind, however, each persuasive in itself, and yet disturbing in that they present
an unresolved clash of organisational philosophy, not fully explained
by industrial circumstances.[10]

Other developments

There are no documents like the Fleck and Herbert reports

to guide understanding of organisational problems in the other nationalised concerns.[11] In the railway industry, however, the changes in organisation have in practice exceeded those elsewhere.

The structure prescribed by the 1947 Act was criticized on several grounds. First, the Transport Commission was too weak and too remote to be able to impose integration on the operating Executives. Secondly, these Executives were each concerned with a particular type of transport, and so were not conducive to integration in their day-to-day working. In the event, the Conservatives' 1953 Act (which abolished the Railway and other Executives) was intended to promote competition rather than improve co-ordination, and for this decentralisation was considered a necessary approach. In 1954 a 'Railways Reorganisation Scheme' was published.[12] It left the London Transport region undisturbed, but set up six Areas in the rest of the country. These were supervised by Area Boards (appointed by the Commission) with executive control in the hands of a chief regional manager. Thus both the Transport Commission and the Area Boards were concerned with policy and supervision, actual management at each level being left to senior officials. In effect, the functions of the old Railways Executive were divided between the Transport Commission itself and the new Area Boards. Other transport activities were devolved to separate managements, though ownership still rested with the Commission.

This structure proved to be temporary. Further reconstruction was brought about in the 1960s by the financial troubles of the railways. The Transport Commission was broken up, the non-railway activities passing to completely independent bodies. The Area Boards of 1954 were renamed Regional Railway Boards, their part-time chairmen to be appointed by the Minister of Transport. They were to have full managerial powers, and the regional general manager was to be a member. Separate regional trading accounts were to provide a basis for testing efficiency. The new Railways Board under Dr Richard Beeching was to 'perform only those central functions which are essential to the running of the railways as a single entity'.

The general argument behind this progressive break-up was that there was no advantage in bringing together functions that are disparate in character and require special handling. The need of the railways was for a policy board that would be able to give attention to commercial viability, as distinct from operating efficiency, and to the future size and shape of the system. This attention could only be given if irrelevant administrative duties were shed. The virtues of regional autonomy were that it fostered rivalry and emulation (though hardly competition in the economic sense) and that it made possible some comparative calculation of efficiency.

The structure of the nationalised gas industry was decentralised from the beginning, and has not been greatly changed. The development of production on a national scale in the 1960s, however, brought about the possibilities of change. It was argued that the import of methane, the construction of a grid, underground storage, and new methods of manufacture would be better carried out by a new central board analogous to the generating board in electricity. In March 1964, however, the Government decided that these functions would continue to be developed by the Gas Council (which is controlled by the chairmen of the Area Gas Boards) and that no further centralisation was necessary.

The discussions about centralisation and decentralisation have usually been couched in practical administrative terms, but it has not been difficult to detect more fundamental attitudes at work. For some the very idea of large unified organisations on a national scale implies bureaucracy and remoteness, and their preference for decentralisation is a protest against bigness in itself. On the other hand, centralisation seems to others to ensure equal treatment for all, including workers and consumers. The trade unions in particular have traditionally favoured basic national rates of pay, so that those who did the same work received roughly the same reward.

At the outset nationalisation was intended, among other things, to bring order and system into confused and diverse industries. For this purpose, and for the change of ownership itself, strong central authority was essential. Moreover, there was at the beginning a considerable shortage of managerial talent and specialist skill, in coalmining especially but in other industries too. Central power was needed to make use of such knowledge as was available, and to see that these qualities were deployed efficiently throughout the industry.

The trend to large-scale operation, and towards the formation of business units comprising many separate undertakings, has proceeded independently of public ownership, and seems to show that in some fields at least there are advantages in central management. In these large private businesses, similar questions of decentralisation arise, and again meet varying solutions. Of course, some public corporations are larger than any private business, but even so, centralised control may still have advantages.

The general administrative factors favouring centralisation in industrial concerns are the need to make careful use of scarce resources — of skill or capital; the need to bring about rapid adaptation to new techniques or new habits of thought; the need to keep some general policy to the forefront; and the desire to maintain national standards and uniformities in some respect, often for the sake of economy. In general terms the things that decentralisation fosters are the development of initiative and the taking of responsibility by many individuals, especially young ones; the opportunity for experiment and new ideas; the closer adaptation of practice to local or special circumstances, and the reduction of interference, reporting, regulation and the like to a minimum.

There are also some economic factors in the discussion. Centralisation, by imposing standardisation and by unifying purchasing and sales practices, enables maximum advantage to be taken of the monopoly power of organisations; and it is argued that this is an advantage yielding material benefits which ought not to be forgone. On the other hand, decentralisation can offer some of the advantages of competition, and even where full competition in the economist's sense does not occur, some rivalry and emulation may be possible.

Two political factors that affect nationalised industries may be added. First, the public corporation is a responsible and accountable body. It has to answer for its actions to the Minister, to Parliament and to the public; its problems in doing so are discussed in Chapter 6. But the existence of such a system means that the central authority — which in the main has to speak for the corporation—must have means of communication with and control over all parts of the industry. Without them it is not in a position to answer, and it cannot make sure that the views it expresses correspond with what is being done in all branches of its organisation. Those who favour decentralisation, therefore, have tended to distrust public account- ability; the Herbert committee, for example, stated that 'if the public insist on having an answer on every point . . . they must put up with the inevitable bureaucracy and rigidity they themselves bring into being.'[13] Wisdom and moderation in these matters may achieve — and have achieved—sensible practices; but the duties of the central boards to the nation must impose some limits on the degree of devolution they permit.

Second, national spirit in Scotland and Wales, and to some extent nationalist politics, make it desirable to set up separate units for those countries if possible. In Scotland the coal industry, railways, electricity, and gas all have independent or autonomous organisa- tions. In Wales not so much is possible. The South-Western division of the Coal Board is largely but not entirely Welsh; the North Wales coalfield is part of the North-Western division. The Western and London Midland Regions of the railways both serve parts of Wales. In electricity there is a South Wales Area Board and one each for Merseyside and North Wales; in gas, how- ever, there is one Area Board for all Wales. The reasons for thes arrangements are technical and geographic (and hence economic), but the treatment of Wales in particular gives rise to some national feeling. Nor does the notion that they are being treated very similarly, in the matter of autonomy, to mere English *regions* arouse much enthusiasm in Celtic hearts.

In spite of the emotions sometimes engendered by different schools of thought, problems of organisation should be capable of settlement on practical grounds. Some advances have been made in recent years in the theoretical study of organisation, and what was once the realm of folklore may eventually be understood in a more scientific way. But it seems prudent to remember that organisations should change: that absence of alteration is likely to mean that there is little dynamism in the industry itself. Thus there may be changes in the balance of centralisation and decentralisation, and they should not be regarded as progressive or retrograde by fixed standards, but in relation to changing needs.

6 Control and Accountability

The effect of nationalisation in practice is to break up the traditional set of ownership rights—rights of use, of access, of disposal, of benefit. Some of these rights have passed to the governing boards of the corporations; others are exercised through the agencies of Government and Parliament.

It is fundamental to the idea of the public corporation that there should be some ministerial control and some public accountability — but not too much. Not surprisingly, it has proved difficult to get these matters arranged to the general satisfaction, and in consequence more words have been written and spoken about this aspect of nationalisation than any other.

There is, of course, a link between control by the Government and accountability to the public. Nevertheless, there is in principle a distinction between the two processes. Control is a purposeful and positive activity, by which definite lines of action are determined. Accountability is an acknowledgment of responsibility, involving the giving of information and explanations about past and current activities. It implies a position of stewardship or of trusteeship on the part of the managers of the undertakings.

MINISTERIAL CONTROL

Each public corporation is controlled by a particular Minister, and it is through his department that the corporation conducts nearly all its relations with the Government. In the case of coal, electricity, and gas, the Minister of Power is responsible; for railways, canals, and associated enterprises, it is the Minister of Transport; and the nationalised airlines are the concern of the Minister of Aviation.

As with organisation, the Nationalisation Acts give some preliminary indication of the situation. The Minister appoints and can
dismiss the members of the boards. Open and persistent defiance of a
Minister may be ruled out, therefore, to begin with. The statutes also
provide for a Minister to give 'directions of a general character . . . in
relation to matters appearing to the Minister to affect the national
interest'.[1] Such directions can be issued only after the Minister has
consulted with the board.

These powers — of appointment, dismissal and direction — provide
a Minister's basic political strength. They are supplemented by
statutory provision on particular topics. The power and transport
corporations (excluding the airlines) must submit schemes of reorganisation, substantial capital development, training, education
and research for the Minister's approval. They must also provide
him with such information as he requires.

Additional matters subject to Government control include the
management of reserve funds or surpluses, and, in electricity and
gas, the definition of Areas.

It should be noted that, besides the relevant Minister, the Treasury
sometimes has the right to be consulted — on the disposal of reserves
and surpluses, on the salaries of board members, on stock issues, and
on the form of the corporations' accounts. The functions of the
Treasury since the war have been such as to make it also a department with a great deal to say about the investment plans of the
industries and other economic aspects of their activities.

The statutes provide at most a skeleton on which flesh and blood
relationships can develop. The main power of general direction has
been little used, and then in exceptional circumstances — to check
further progress into steel nationalisation when the Conservatives
came to power in 1951, for example, or to limit rises in passenger
fares on the railways in 1952. Even with the subjects of the specific
legal powers listed above, experience now provides a much better
guide to the realities of the relationship than does the text of the
Acts.

Do these legal stipulations express the full intentions of the
nationalisers? It may be suspected that two factors were at work.

First, there was a clear desire that an elected Government should be allowed to have its way: the public corporations were not to be allowed to become independent powers in the country, able to ignore the political will of the electors, as formulated by the Government of the day. This was almost the sole motive in nationalising the Bank of England, and its effect on the other corporations lay in the provisions for definite political supremacy. There is no indication, however, of any clear ideas about how often such political intervention would be needed, or how close an interest a Minister would take in the affairs of a corporation. The experience of pre-war public corporations seemed to indicate that what might be needed was an occasional veto, or the setting of a new policy line now and again. Nevertheless, the deep political interest in the affairs of the newly nationalised industries could have suggested that such a degree of abstention would not be practicable.

A second factor was the type of Government policy necessary to maintain full employment. This had its statutory expression in the rule about approval of investment plans. Labour Party economists tended to believe, moreover, that the public sector of the economy, if large enough, could be used to maintain a high rate of activity. The industrial public corporations were expected to play a key part in this, and hence a Government's economic planners would need control more intimate than that which had existed before the war.

At all events, a system of regular contacts between the heads of the nationalised industries and Ministers soon grew up. There were from the beginning urgent national problems — of fuel shortage, for example — which made close co-operation desirable, and Ministers found that they needed to be well informed to cope with public criticism. Constant involvement in practice meant high-level, if informal, policy discussions. Mr G. R. Strauss has explained that, when Minister of Supply, he had weekly talks with the chairman and deputy-chairman of the Iron and Steel Corporation, and they discussed 'every single problem, not only of national interest but on every conceivable detail concerning that Corporation. There was not a subject with which I was not concerned.'[2] This is not to say, of course, that a Minister uses the meetings to impose his views: there is no doubt a process of mutual influence and consultation. Nor need the process be as frequent or as detailed for other industries as in the example given by Mr Strauss. There is no doubt, however, that procedures of the same type existed, and continue to exist, for all the main industrial public corporations.

The contacts between Government and public corporations are not confined to the top level. Civil servants keep in touch with the staff of the corporations on many matters, routine and occasional. Government departments are expected to accumulate their own knowledge and understanding of particular industries, in order to form disinterested judgments about industrial problems. But though their views may eventually differ from those held inside the corporations, the building up of information and comprehension can be done only by co-operation with those working directly on the affairs of the industry.

It must be accepted, therefore, that the Government exerts a pervasive influence on the policies of the nationalised industries. On what subjects is this influence most apparent? Four categories may be indicated:

(a) The general forward planning of the industry is clearly one such matter. The statutory powers of the Minister in relation to investment, finance, research, and training are all focused in this direction, and, even if they did not exist, any Government that had to take responsibility for economic prosperity would want to assure itself about the prospects for the basic industries. In addition to Government departments, the National Economic Development Council has, since 1962, been concerned with economic growth and future prosperity. The chairmen of the National Coal Board and the Electricity Council are members of the N.E.D.C., and the staff of its office consult directly with all the corporations as they prepare their prognostications.

The financial troubles in which many of the newly nationalised industries found themselves made further consultations necessary. The deficits incurred made the financing of investment programmes exceptionally difficult, and again the statutory requirements were reinforced by practical necessities, obliging all concerned to co-ordinate their activities.

(b) The central financial aspect of a corporation's business is the price at which it sells its products. (The proper criteria for fixing prices are discussed in Chapter 7.) It cannot be emphasised too strongly, however, that all appreciable changes in price levels by nationalised industries are discussed with the Government. For significant changes the issue may go beyond the particular department controlling the industry, and be taken up by the Treasury or even the Cabinet. It is acknowledged that a 'gentleman's agreement' exists—dating from wartime conditions in the coal industry—whereby the boards submit proposed price changes for the Minister's information or even approval. The process is normally a confidential one, and the cases quoted below are instances of exceptional public knowledge of the situation. The responsibility for the changes, including their form, extent, and consequences, must remain with the public corporations, save when some public declaration is made to the contrary. (For the effect of the White Paper of 1961, see below, p. 120.)

There are some well established cases where price rises are known to have been modified, delayed, or amended by Government action. For example, in 1955 the prospect of mounting losses caused the National Coal Board to propose a substantial rise in the price of coal. The rise was delayed for four months by the Minister of Power, and though an even larger rise was then made, the N.C.B. incurred a heavy loss that year.[3] (See p. 70.) In 1956 the Minister of Transport revised, and effectively reduced, rises in charges proposed by the British Transport Commission, even after they had been approved by the Transport Tribunal—again with serious effects on the industry's financial position.[4] These are examples only, showing direct intervention. Whether specific alterations come to light or not, the process of consultation on prices persists. In 1965 the Labour Government set up a National Board for Prices and Incomes, to help work out a national incomes policy, and in consequence proposals for price increases by nationalised industries may be referred to this body.

(c) Wage negotiation is another subject of major Government interest; and here the extent of intervention is at its most obscure and controversial. Negotiations take place between the corporations, as employers, and the trade unions representing the employees, and formally the Government takes no part. Yet in fact there is no doubt that the views of the Government are made known to the corporations, and their negotiators can hardly fail to take these into account. If the corporation is in a weak financial condition, it will be in no position to ignore such pressure. If a rise in labour costs cannot be absorbed, then prices will have to be raised, which, under the 'gentleman's agreement', will require Government approval. Further, in cases such as the railways, where higher charges might not bring in greater revenue, then a subsidy may be necessary. In such a situation the Government's part is indispensable, and more open.

Usually, however, the Government stays in the background, and much resentment is expressed by trade unionists at this situation. They complain that they are negotiating only with shadows, and that the true 'paymasters' do not come forward. However, it cannot be denied that the corporations are the employers and must take a large part in wage settlements. On at least one occasion they have acted contrary to Government advice, for the Electricity Council was publicly rebuked by the Prime Minister in November 1961 for granting an increase in excess of what the Government thought justifiable.[5]

Nevertheless, the general position of the Government in wage negotiations is ambiguous. Clearly it expects to have its views respected, and hitherto it has seemed to assume that its rights inside the 'public sector' are greater than outside it. If a Government wants *special* influence over these settlements, however, then there is surely a case for its being openly represented in negotiations, and for making its attitude clear at the outset.

(d) These three broad categories of Government influence should not obscure the wide range of topics actually discussed. In addition to plans, prices, and wage settlements, a miscellany of particular topics is considered—the siting of power stations, land for opencast mining, air-charter policy, and so on. The Government is also known to exert influence in order to maintain various uneconomic activities. A classic case is the air service in the Highlands and islands of Scotland provided by British European Airways, which always makes a loss, borne by the corporation.

In April 1961 the Conservative Government published a White Paper setting new general policies for the nationalised industries. This document, *Financial and Economic Obligations of the Nationalised Industries*,[6] contained several propositions discussed in this chapter and the next. Here it should be noted that the White Paper, and subsequent action, set new standards and new principles by Government decision alone. There was no legislation. The White Paper was drawn up by the Government, in consultation with the corporations in the usual manner. Its effectiveness as a determinant of the general framework of policy illustrates the power of the system of ministerial control that has grown up.

In sum, on a great range of problems there is discussion between the Government and the public corporations. Apart from generalities, decisions on the problems rest with the boards of the corporations. The regular contacts mean, however, that the boards are open to much persuasion: they may be subject to influence; they may be vulnerable to pressure, and they can be threatened with direction—though the actual use of powers of direction remains highly exceptional.

Too much control?

In the nationalised industries the influence of the Ministers has increased and is increasing. Ought it to be diminished?

It should be emphasised that the influence is not necessarily one-way. Indeed, if the object of informing the Minister is to help him meet criticisms in Parliament, or in his own department, then the balance of advantage may be with the corporations. On most specialised topics the expertise available in the industries should be sufficient for their actions to be defended successfully. As a matter of personality, too, a determined board chairman may find it possible to persuade an average Minister even more often than he is persuaded by him. In day-to-day terms there is undoubtedly a two-way process of influence. Nevertheless, the ultimate, legal, powers lie with the Government, and their presence cannot fail to sway many situations.

It should be remembered that private industry also has close relations with Government departments, either through trade associations or directly. Here again there is a process of mutual persuasion. The oil companies are believed to inform the Ministry of Power about prospective price changes; and if they do, the Minister can easily put considerations before the companies about these changes. But this is an exceptional, and in any case a voluntary, arrangement. In principle the powers and responsibilities of Ministers *vis-à-vis* private firms are very different, and so the means of influencing them must also be very different.

On occasions the relationship between Minister and public corporation has been described in doubtful terms. A well-known example is the statement made in March 1953 by Lord Swinton in the House of Lords, to the effect that 'the Minister's day-to-day contact with the chairman of a nationalised board is very like one's relationship with one's own officials in one's department.'[7] Again, in the White Paper on the *Reorganisation of National Transport Undertakings* of 1960, a chart shows the Minister of Transport at the head of a new structure, with responsibilities for overall co-ordination and general efficiency.[8]

These formulations, literally interpreted, are a travesty of the original conception of the public corporation. The Minister has certain very strong powers in relation to a public corporation, but he was not intended to control it in the way he controls his own department. Moreover, his functions relate to policy rather than efficiency. A public corporation cannot be expected to operate properly where these misunderstandings of its status prevail.

The general motives that impel Governments to take such a close interest in the affairs of corporations should be remembered in this context. The supervision of plans, about which there is little controversy, is at the heart of the matter: and the need for it arises from the Government's responsibilities—unavoidable in the twentieth century—for national economic well-being. This responsibility for the national economy also explains the Government's interest in prices and wage settlements. The miscellaneous matters are supervised for more political motives—the need of the Government to meet questions and criticisms about the general activities of the corporations. Thus it is usually its care for the economy that has led the Government to threaten the independence of the corporations; and in particular the notion of the 'public sector' as a sphere in which the Government had direct powers of control has meant drastic limitations on the corporations' autonomy. In the 1960s an attempt has begun to build a system of economic planning on a wider basis, and if this succeeds, then special control over the investment, prices and wages of the nationalised industries may no longer be desired. Even so, the nationalised industries are mainly basic industries on which the rest of the economy depends. As such they are naturally subject to close Government attention, whatever their formal status.

If these are the Government's motives, then what accounts for the acceptance of the situation by the public corporations? In the background, of course, are the formidable legal powers of the Minister, and the urgencies of past crises have bred habits that have persisted. Public corporations are obliged to give information, and it is therefore difficult to refuse to discuss problems arising from the facts. If there is man-to-man discussion, then compromises, accommodations and mutual understandings arise naturally. It is thus the informality, the casualness even, of the situation that makes it difficult for the boards.

There are two main lines of criticism of ministerial control. The first condemns its extent, the second its secrecy.

The causes of ministerial intervention have been explained. There does not seem to be any prospect of the general causes diminishing in importance—the Government will still be concerned with national prosperity and with meeting criticisms. If the corporations can free themselves from financial difficulties, particularly on current trading, however, there could be some relaxation of pressure. This improvement depends itself largely on Government policy about public-enterprise prices, of course, but there now seems some prospect of an economic level of charges being maintained, according to the 1961 White Paper.[9] Financial matters are far from being the only subject of Government interest, and improvement would not necessarily lessen contacts; but it would strengthen the hand of the corporations in those contacts.

Frequent or infrequent, however, these contacts are informal and private. Though many levels of administrators are involved, the key relationship lies between the Minister and the board chairman. Since it is personal and confidential, no formal decisions can be reached. In any case, the Minister is but one member of the Government, and the chairman must carry his board with him. Nevertheless, there is here more than a channel of communication: there is a policy-making nexus of some sort.

If this were all, it might not matter very much. Ministers are well advised to keep in close touch with leading personalities within their field of responsibilities. The issue is whether the responsibility for decisions is obscured by the system. Perhaps there is some hope of greater clarity. The 1961 White Paper stated: 'If a Board decided to modify their own proposals [on prices] by reason of views expressed by the Minister, it would be open to them to require a written statement of those views, which could be published by the Minister or the Board . . .' A good deal depends on how this operates in practice. It does not mean that there will be, necessarily, a published statement: it depends on whether the board (or perhaps the Minister) wants one or not. There is no acknowledgment that outsiders have any right to information if the parties to the agreement prefer not to give it; and in any case the statement relates only to prices.[10]

The outlook for greater publicity, therefore, is only mildly encouraging. Much of British government is conducted in conditions of privacy, and as a matter of personal confidence. The arrangements for control of public corporations are in line with this state of affairs, and it is in this general situation that the roots of the system must be sought, rather than in the particular circumstances of nationalised industries. In British government the counterbalance to secret policy-making is allegedly provided by thorough arrangements for accountability to Parliament and public, and the working of this system for nationalisation must now be examined.

ACCOUNTABILITY TO PARLIAMENT

If the pre-war public corporations were subject to little control by ministers, their accountability to Parliament was virtually non-existent. The strengthening of Government control over the post-war corporations was expected to carry with it closer parliamentary interest. This interest was thought to be catered for automatically under the conventions of ministerial responsibility. The theory of the public corporations' accountability to Parliament was simple and logical. The Minister had certain powers over the corporations. For the exercise of these powers he was answerable to Parliament, just as he was answerable for all his other powers. On those matters where the Minister exercised no powers, there was no accountability. This would correspond with the extent of the corporations' managerial independence. In so far as the post-war corporations were under greater ministerial control, so parliamentary discussion could be greater too; but all depended on the Minister, and the possibility of accountability depended essentially on him. In practice this was expected to mean that Parliament could discuss 'broad policy' but not 'day-to-day management'.

This technique of accountability did not weather parliamentary storms very well, and modifications have now been introduced. Their nature can best be understood if the means of information and debate available to Parliament are reviewed.

Three different methods may be distinguished: debates, questions, and select committees.

Debates on the affairs of nationalised industries may arise in several different ways. Sometimes there is important legislation concerning an industry, perhaps revising its whole structure —the Electricity Act 1957, for example. The passing of such measures obviously gives rise to extensive discussion; and though for any particular industry they may occur rarely, in fact there is some legislation concerning the public corporations almost every year. Secondly, the annual reports and accounts of each industry are presented to Parliament by the Minister responsible. Not every industry is properly debated every year, but two or three are chosen annually for full discussion. Thirdly, other opportunities may be taken to start debates—the Opposition may find time, on one of the days when it has choice of subject; or private members may use their special opportunities; and the debate at the beginning of each session when there is a general review of Government policy may contain reflections on these industries.[11] The Government itself may find it opportune to move a motion concerning a nationalised industry. Economic and financial matters provide other opportunities— the annual White Papers on *Public Investment* and *Loans from the Consolidated Fund* may be debated, and from time to time public corporations wish to raise the statutory limit on their borrowing powers, which can only be done by legislation.

This may seem a formidable list. But in fact, debates on the annual reports are the only regular general discussions; and some industries may pass several years without being examined in this way. In any case, only limited aspects of the work of the corporations are likely to be raised, often those which have caught the popular notice. On the floor of the House of Commons, too, partisan attitudes are at the fore, and little light may emerge even from lengthy exchanges. In debates the nationalised industries cannot be directly represented, but in a sense Ministers speak on their behalf. Since public corporations are not the same as departments, this is not entirely satisfactory. What Ministers defend is the Government's attitude to the nationalised industries, and this may not be quite the same thing as defending the nationalised industries.

Debates may also take place in the House of Lords, where procedure is flexible and general motions on the industries can be discussed. Legislation, of course, must go through the usual stages in the Lords.

The story of parliamentary questions on the nationalised industries shows most clearly the difficulties of maintaining the original theory of accountability. At first, indeed, nationalisation had the unexpected effect of removing some matters from parliamentary scrutiny. The railways, for example, had been taken over by the Government during the war, and Ministers had answered questions — on points of some detail — about their running. Transference to a public corporation, therefore, took them out of the Minister's emergency control, and, in accordance with the theory of managerial independence, questions on details were refused an answer.

In spite of this embarrassment, Ministers set out to maintain a fairly strict rule about questions. Questions were allowed only on matters that were the Minister's responsibility, and it was primarily for him to acknowledge what was his responsibility and what was not. When he had indicated subjects he considered to be outside his responsibilities, officials of the House of Commons then refused to accept further questions on those subjects. One modification only has been made to this rule. In 1948 the Minister of Fuel and Power refused to answer questions about electricity load-shedding, as this was for the Electricity Authority to deal with, not a matter of general policy. Officials of the House of Commons noted this refusal, and accepted no more questions. But the electricity situation worsened, load-shedding became frequent and obviously a matter of national importance. It was impossible to keep the subject out of parliamentary discussion. In June 1948, therefore, the Speaker announced that subjects on which answers had been refused could nevertheless be raised, by question, if he considered them of sufficient public importance. Since 1948 the rule has been maintained virtually without change. In spite of their early criticisms, the Conservatives made no substantial alteration when they came to power in 1951. Later statements of the rule are merely reformulations and make no difference.

Two practical developments, however, have made the operation of the rule less onerous than it might seem. At a very early stage Ministers found it possible to give information while not accepting (or even explicitly denying) any responsibility, by prefacing their answers with, 'I am informed by the board that . . .', or some such formula. This creates a degree of flexibility for the Ministers, though it does not mean that they are bound to provide information on any topic. Secondly, Members of Parliament have developed techniques for avoiding the rule. Questions may be asked about a Minister's responsibilities, not merely his positive actions. It is therefore possible to ask why he has *not* taken action on a particular matter. To make certain, a Member may ask why the Minister has not issued a general direction on the point: and clearly this is a question relating to the Minister's powers, which must be answered. By this and similar methods a considerable range of questions can be asked, and once the topic is aired, further implications may be drawn out by means of supplementary questions.

There is thus a gap between the rigid principle and the actual working of parliamentary questioning. What is in fact possible may be indicated by examples from the session 1961-2, when questions were asked and answered on coal prices, pit closures, and the chemical uses of coal; underground transmission of electricity; the reading of electricity and gas meters; capital expenditure by an Area gas board; underground storage of gas, and railway branch-line closures. By asking for a 'general direction', the advertising of electricity boards and prices in railway catering establishments were raised. Other factual information was given by written answers.

The case for more questions is simply that the corporations are public bodies, and public bodies should be open to scrutiny whatever their strict constitutional position. Members of Parliament with constituencies in which the nationalised industries operate are particularly anxious to raise local grievances. The case against detailed questioning depends partly on constitutional principle and partly on the needs of industrial management. The right to question should be, constitutionally, conterminous with the responsibilities of the Minister — to widen the scope of questions would widen his responsibilities and automatically destroy the independence of the public corporations. It would make the corporations operate like the Civil Service, and would be inimical to efficiency. It would lead to over-centralisation, too much record-keeping, and excessive caution—in short, the need to have an answer to all possible questions would inhibit initiative and risk-taking.

The outcome of these conflicting considerations is a situation of some confusion. It is difficult to see how the rule could be altered, given the assumption of managerial autonomy for the corporations. Yet ways are found in practice of avoiding it, and it is hard to believe that it provides an easy guide for a Minister who has to decide whether a question should be answered or not. Attempts to secure greater rights for Members of Parliament recur, but parliamentary scrutiny has concentrated in recent years on a more powerful and searching instrument than the question: the select committee.

A select committee of the House of Commons is a group of Members, usually small, appointed by the House to carry out reviews and investigations on general aspects of Government activity. Its membership reflects the party balance in the House of Commons itself. It has power to call for written evidence and to question witnesses; but its duty is merely to report to the House—it has no independent authority. The select committees regularly appointed by the House include one on delegated legislation and two on Government finance, the Estimates Committee and the Public Accounts Committee.

The Public Accounts Committee has the function of examining the accounts of Government departments and other public bodies, to ensure that money is being properly and economically spent. The accounts of the public corporations fall within its terms of reference, and for some years there were tentative examinations of these accounts. At first it took evidence mainly from civil servants whose duties included contact with the nationalised industries. In 1951-2 it took evidence from the auditors of the accounts of the British Transport Commission, two eminent commercial accountants. The work of the committee, however, was hesitant and not very searching. It was hampered by lack of expert guidance, and the committee was reluctant to give the time from its already full programme that a really thorough examination would require.

In fact, it was doubtful if the Public Accounts Committee was an appropriate body for such inquiries. If the work was to be done

properly, then a special body concerned with the nationalised
industries as such was required. Such a body was early proposed by a
Labour M.P., Mr J. Baird, and was extensively canvassed by a
Conservative Member, Mr Hugh Molson (now Lord Molson). But
before the Select Committee on Nationalised Industries was
successfully launched, there were many doubts and difficulties and
one false start.

The nature of the doubts has already been indicated: they
centred on the undesirability of subjecting the 'business' or 'commercial' style of management, appropriate to the nationalised
industries, to constant probing and detailed criticism. Many evils
were alleged to arise from such investigation — bureaucracy, centralisation, and lack of enterprise being the most frequently cited.
The statement of Lord Heyworth, the chairman of Unilever Ltd,
expressed the situation of the industrial manager very forcefully,
and indeed has become something of a classic.

> I look upon myself as someone who is perpetually in a fog . . .
> If people came to look at everything I did in a year after the
> events, the shareholders would be horrified because they
> would see that some of my decisions were quite wrong. The
> more I felt that someone was looking over my shoulder all the
> time and was going to examine these things at any time later,
> the less I would be inclined to take a decision, the less decisive
> I would become, and pretty well certainly the less good would
> be the results.[12]

This view from a successful private businessman was reinforced by
similar fears expressed by the existing chairmen of nationalised
industries. Nevertheless, one chairman, Lord Hurcomb of the Transport Commission, thought that some sort of parliamentary committee might be useful, and in 1953 a committee of the House of
Commons reported in favour of establishing a committee to
examine the nationalised industries, with the object of '. . . informing
Parliament about the aims, activities and problems of the Corporations and not of controlling their work'.[13]

The first Select Committee on Nationalised Industries, set up in

1955, was abortive. In its terms of reference precise limits were set to what it could do, and it was prohibited from examining anything that was a ministerial responsibility, anything to do with collective bargaining, or anything that was a matter of day-to-day management. Nevertheless, it was to consider the *current* activities of the corporations. After a few months of trying to find something useful to do, the committee reported that nothing worth while could be done within its terms of reference.

In May 1956 the Government agreed to set up a new committee; at the end of November a motion to set it up was moved by Mr R. A. Butler. The Labour Party opposed the motion, Mr James Callaghan arguing that such a committee would blur the chain of responsibility from the boards to Ministers. The motion was carried, the committee was appointed in December and began work in February 1957.

The Select Committee on Nationalised Industries (Reports and Accounts) has the following terms of reference:

> ... to examine the Reports and Accounts of the Nationalised Industries established by Statute whose controlling Boards are appointed by Ministers of the Crown and whose annual receipts are not wholly or mainly derived from moneys provided by Parliament or advanced by the Exchequer.

There are thus no restrictive limitations on its work: it is left to the committee itself to choose its subjects of inquiry and to conduct its investigations in a reasonable manner. The corporations subject to its surveillance are the trading bodies: thus the B.B.C. and the Atomic Energy Authority are excluded, and so are undertakings owned or partly owned by the Government which are not public corporations, such as Cable and Wireless Ltd, British Petroleum Ltd, and Richard Thomas and Baldwins Ltd. There are thirteen members of the committee, and it has so far conducted its affairs in an entirely non-partisan manner, its reports being unanimous. It calls for and examines written memoranda, and questions witnesses orally—civil servants, members of the boards, and staff of the corporations.

It has come to be the practice for one or two major reports to appear annually, and for the committee to investigate each nationalised industry in turn, rather than look into topics (e.g. pricing policies) that would concern all the industries.

The first subjects of the S.C.N.I.'s investigations, in 1957, were ministerial control, including Treasury influence, and the North of Scotland Hydro-Electric Board. On the first, not much illumination was provided; on the Hydro-Electric Board it found that 'in the fourteen years of its existence [it] has impressively justified the faith of its progenitors'.[14] It then turned to a more formidable subject, the National Coal Board, and its report of 1958 threw much light on the effect of Government-imposed policies about exports, imports of American coal, and prices, on the Board's financial performance. The committee's 1959 report followed a thorough investigation of the nationalised airlines. It contained some praise and some criticism, particularly of maintenance costs. The long 1960 report, which included fifty-six factual appendices, dealt with British railways, and found much to criticise in their costing and policy judgments, though the committee had no doubt that a large-scale British railways system could be profitable. The gas industry was reviewed in the 1961 report, and the committee stressed the need for lower costs of production and for more research to that end.

In 1962 a very full report on electricity was published, the first outside investigation since the reorganisation of 1957. In 1963 the committee reported on a number of investigations it had made into the consequences of its previous recommendations. Its main subject in 1964 was the British Overseas Airways Corporation, but it also produced special reports on gas and electricity.

The S.C.N.I. is generally considered to be a very successful body. The nationalised industries have accepted it with good grace and regard it as a very useful link with Parliament and with the informed public. There is little doubt that the general understanding of Members has been improved by its reports, and that their debates are more enlightened as a result of the committee's influence. The atmosphere of discussion on nationalisation is, between election campaigns, more moderate, constructive and well informed. Their reports and proceedings constitute first-class material for the research worker. In some degree this acceptance is due to the political restraint of the committee. It concentrates on the evidence put before it and the inferences to be drawn from it. Conservative members of the committee do not condemn weaknesses as inherent in the principle of nationalisation, nor do Labour members try to extol its successes as springing from that very principle. Their reports, therefore, light no fires of party controversy.

These are considerable achievements; yet their extent and their nature should be noted. Sir Toby Low (now Lord Aldington), a former chairman, has pointed out that the S.C.N.I. 'has but to unravel the facts and point the moral. Others take the action.'[15] The morals pointed by the committee have sometimes been the guide for action; but often they have not. The Government continues to appoint special committees to advise it—the Stedeford committee on the railways and the Corbett report on British Overseas Airways were more powerful instigators of policy than any S.C.N.I. report. The general views of the committee—on ministerial intervention taking place by published directions, and on the provision of subsidies for uneconomic services—have been rejected.

It must also be remembered that the S.C.N.I. is very lightly staffed. During the discussions before it was set up, there were suggestions that it should have expert help, and an official similar to the Comptroller and Auditor General was proposed.[16] But in fact no office of comparable skill and power has been set up. When the S.C.N.I. began, it was arranged for it to have the assistance of senior Treasury civil servants who were concerned with aspects of the nationalised industries in their normal work. This was not very successful, and most of the work of the committee has been done with the assistance of one or two clerks—that is to say, officials of the House of Commons, including eventually a statistician. In July 1959 the committee produced a special report in which they asked for the services of an accountant and an economist, and the staff of the committee was augmented as a result.[17] So far, however, the

I

committee has not had the power to recruit, or hire, the services of experts who are not on the staff of the House of Commons. The committee does not provide a rigorous examination of the efficiency of all parts of the industries: '. . . it was not our duty to go into their day-to-day activities; it was not our duty to make an efficiency or financial audit; neither was it our duty to check in detail the rightness or wrongness of technical decisions and so on.'[18]

The success of the S.C.N.I. does not refute the arguments of those who feared detailed examination of day-to-day management; on the contrary, its achievements have been made possible by its restraint and its refusal to pursue minor points. Its function, in short, is to provide a clear explanation, in non-technical language, of the problems of the industries, accompanied by shrewd comments and criticisms.

Further accountability

Should something more be done? The assistance provided for the S.C.N.I. is modest, and raises the question of whether more formidable investigations should take place.

The efficiency audit is a widely canvassed proposal of this nature. There are several versions, but in all there is essentially a body of expert assessors—cost accountants, management consultants, production engineers, and the like—who would carry out thorough examinations of aspects of the work of the industries. Professor W. A. Robson would have this done by an 'audit commission', with its reports available to the S.C.N.I.; Professor Sargant Florence and Mr Henry Maddick connect it with the work of consumer councils; Lord Morrison suggested that the public corporations themselves should control such a unit. In any case it would provide more than general comments on policies: it would provide specialist scrutiny, and measurement where possible, of the actual operations of the industries, in whole or in part. If constituted as a permanent body, it would acquire a knowledge and understanding of public enterprise which could lend great authority to its views.

This proposal has been strongly resisted by the boards, who

regard the measurement of efficiency in this way as a function of management, not of external accountability. An audit unit, they believe, would become a fault-finding and perfectionist body in order to justify its own existence, and it would undermine the morale of management if outsiders professing superior skill were imposed upon them for the purpose of publishing criticisms.

There is no doubt some psychological truth in this attitude. But the assessment of efficiency could make a vital contribution to public accountability, and if the boards insist on its being an internal function, then the reports and surveys that emerge should be available at least to the Select Committee on Nationalised Industries.

Another scheme of public accountability, which was canvassed in the 1950s, was the periodic committee of inquiry. This was the method approved by the Labour Party. At first, intervals of seven years between inquiries for each industry were proposed, but in the policy document *Public Enterprise* of 1957, this was lengthened to ten years. The investigations would be conducted by Government committees constituted in the normal way: that is, varied and balanced sets of individuals chosen by a Minister, fresh for each inquiry. This is the system by which the broadcasting authorities, the B.B.C. and the I.T.A., are examined. It has not been applied methodically to industrial undertakings, though some inquiries have taken place which follow the principle roughly — the Chambers committee on London Transport (1955), the Herbert committee on electricity (1956), and the Mackenzie committee on Scottish electricity (1962). There have also been unpublished reports. The nationalised industries were not enamoured of this proposal either, especially if the inquiries were to take place at short intervals without any clear purpose, since such investigations take up a great deal of the boards' time and trouble. The successful establishment of the S.C.N.I. does not rule out these special inquiries, but it probably ensures that they will take place only when the Government has some definite purpose in mind, beyond general review.

All accountability is based on the presentation of information. It should not be forgotten that the public corporations are obliged by statute to publish extensive reports and accounts annually.

These take the form of documents submitted to the relevant Minister, and are in turn presented by him to Parliament. Their scope and contents form the starting point of the inquiries of the S.C.N.I. The real strength of the system lies, however, in the fact that reports and accounts are published: and so a great amount of information, statistical and descriptive, is made available to all.

The report reviews the general financial and economic positions of the industry, including its sales and marketing problems; describes its production, its productivity, and its technical advance during the year; gives an account of labour relations and personnel matters, and discusses research and training progress. Some are embellished with photographs. The accounts not only cover financial matters but also include non-monetary statistics of production, manpower, technical efficiency, and so on. Apart from the usual balance sheet and some other financial accounts, most information is presented in tabular form rather than as two-sided accounts. The first object of the accounts is to give a general view of the state of the industry; these main accounts are then supported and explained by schedules; and notes on the accounts explain the methods used (e.g. for valuing stocks) to arrive at the figures. Special accounts for particular activities and sub-units are given, and tables are provided showing developments in production, profits or losses, and so on, over ten-year or similar periods. Annual reports of the main nationalised industries are usually documents of some forty to eighty pages, and the accounts are of similar length.

In finding out about the nationalised industries, perhaps the critics neglect the most obvious way. This is to communicate directly: to write a letter, or even to arrange an interview. No doubt there is a limit to the trouble staff can be expected to take, and some information which for commercial reasons they will not divulge. But in general, requests for information receive helpful replies. Nothing is more annoying to the public corporations in discussions of accountability than the assumption that, without parliamentary questions or statutory compulsions, no information would be available. There is, of course, more to accountability than information. Where facts are needed, however, the simplest course for Members of Parliament and private citizens alike is to write directly to the board's head-quarters. A considerable correspondence is in practice dealt with throughout the year, and when parliamentary debates are in prospect many M.P.s are supplied with information, on the Opposition as well as the Government side. No official doctrine about the relations between a public corporation and the Opposition in Parliament has ever been formulated, but it seems that (if the boards choose) greater freedom is possible than for civil servants.

All the main nationalised industries have public relations and Press departments through which they try to spread understanding of their activities and to build up the public reputation of their own industry. Some of the industries, such as coal and the railways, have large labour forces who are liable to be influenced by the image presented by the mass media. It is important, therefore, for the self-confidence of the industries as well as for their external standing, that the impact of publicity be favourable. Most industries advertise for sales and recruitment purposes as well as prestige. London Transport acquired an early reputation for the high quality of its posters and publicity material, and in recent years advertising slogans like 'Progressive Industry is going forward on Coal', 'High-Speed Gas', and 'It's quicker by Rail' have become as familiar as their private-enterprise counterparts.

Whatever its merits, publicity is not accountability, and a special aspect of the responsibility of the corporations remains to be covered.

CONSUMERS' REPRESENTATION

Though the Labour Government of 1945–51 accepted the theory of the managerial public corporation, it was sensitive to the interests which had been baulked of representation on the boards. It therefore provided in the statutes for compulsory collective bargaining and joint consultation with the workers in the industries. It also set up machinery for the representation of consumers' interests.

At one time it was thought that the Government itself, being democratically elected, was an appropriate spokesman for the consumer. The pressures on Government action, and the motives behind it, however, are many, and in practice the interests of producers and its own political concerns have usually been to the fore. Since consumers are numerous, it is reasonable to regard relations with them as an aspect of accountability to the public: but since as consumers their interests are of a specific type, it is right that special machinery should be available to express their views. For the main nationalised industries, with the exception of the air corporations, consumers' councils or consultative councils were established. In the coal industry there are two: the Industrial Coal Consumers' Council and the Domestic Coal Consumers' Council. In electricity there is a consultative council in each Area, fourteen in all. There are also twelve gas consultative councils in the Areas. In transport there is a Central Transport Consultative Committee, as well as Transport Users' Consultative Committees for Scotland, Wales, and nine English Areas.

The number of members of each committee is about twenty, and they are all appointed by the relevant Minister. Otherwise there are considerable variations in administrative practice. The coal councils are financed by the Ministry of Power, which provides administrative staff; in other cases expenses and staff are provided by the corporations. Frequency of meetings varies between eight a year for some gas or electricity councils, and sometimes only four for the transport committees. On the coal councils there are at least two representatives of the National Coal Board; in electricity and gas the chairman of the consultative council is ex officio a member of the Area Board. Since 1962 the transport consultative committees, however, have had no representatives of the public corporations as members.

The selection of members by the Minister to represent the consuming public has given rise to some problems. The usual method is to ask organised interest groups to suggest names, from which the Minister chooses individuals. However, some interests are not conveniently organised (domestic coal consumers, railway passengers), and there must be resort to local authorities and women's organisations. These can suggest public-spirited individuals, but there is no guarantee that they have any particular background knowledge of the market or of consumers' affairs.

The purpose of these councils and committees is to make recommendations to the boards about consumers' needs, and to develop mutual understanding between suppliers and customers. Their field of interest lies between that of broad policy and that of petty grievances. When they were first established, they tended to discourage individual complaints; the general practice now is to insist that customers with grievances should first approach the management of the boards directly, but after continued dissatisfaction the councils are prepared to take up issues. The councils do not want to become general complaints bureaux, but they are open as channels of appeal, and it is obviously desirable that they should deal with the serious grievances of consumers. In fact the various councils now take up some thousands of complaints annually. Again, there is no point in spending time voicing obvious truisms, such as that consumers want lower prices. The reasons for increases, however, are explained to councils, and the structure of tariffs is discussed. Inefficiencies and waste which come to the notice of consumers can be brought to the attention of the boards. Standards and methods of service are, after prices, the main topic of interest. One of the difficulties of the Domestic Coal Consumers' Council is that the National Coal Board is normally not in direct touch with domestic consumers. There are some coal merchants on the council, but they are not in a position to redress complaints about other firms. Moreover, in these circumstances it is not easy to be sure in a particular matter how far the Coal Board may be at fault and how far the merchant.

The most significant work of the transport committees has been concerned with railway closures. It has been the practice for each proposed closure to be considered by the appropriate Transport Users' Consultative Committee. Objectors may appear before the committee, and the committee reports to the Minister of Transport, who makes the final decision. In these cases the committees are acting more in the role of public inquiries than as normal councils. In 1962 their structure was modified (the representatives of the railways being omitted), and a definite procedure for the cases was laid down. The duties of the committees are confined to reporting on hardship —how much would arise from a closure and how it might be alleviated. They do not go into the financial background, which is the prerogative of the railway management.

The impact of consumers' representation on the community has not been exciting. Many criticisms have been made of the system. First, it has been said that the relations between the corporations and the consumers' councils have been too close and too good. It should not be the function of a transport users' committee to assess fairly the arguments about branch-line closures—the committee should be the body that marshals the consumers' case before some other authority. The presence of board representatives on some councils has been particularly criticised; their expertise gives them a great advantage in discussion, and in any case their presence makes the councils moderate and impartial bodies instead of partisans of the consumers.

Secondly, the very existence of the councils is not widely known, and their complex structure makes it difficult for a consumer to understand them. Again, their reasonableness deters them from attracting publicity to themselves. The position, as shown by the number of complaints received, seems to be improving, and no doubt will continue to do so.

Thirdly, the councils have too little money, too few staff and too little knowledge. They are in no position to challenge the boards' experts; they can only present a layman's view. Schemes have been put forward to strengthen them in this respect, including a plan to make them responsible for efficiency audits. More modest proposals concentrate on strengthening the secretariats of the councils.

The fundamental problem for consumer councils, however, lies in their relationship with their clientele, the consumers. The members owe their positions to appointment by the Minister, and the councils have had to cultivate relations with the public. There was no great popular demand for them at their inception, and at their worst they seemed like heads without bodies, looking after the interests of people who were unaware of this protection. In the 1960s, however, a widely based movement for consumer protection gathered strength, and resulted in greater public interest in consumer matters. A new, official Consumer Council was created in 1963, not attached to any enterprise but concerned with consumers' interests in general. These developments may provide what the machinery for consumers' representation in nationalised industry most needs – popular backing and pressure. They are then likely to obtain the resources of staff and expertise they require, because the need for them will be manifest.

Some other bodies concerned with the regulation of public enterprise may be mentioned here for the sake of completeness. The Transport Act of 1947 established the Transport Tribunal (in succession to a Railway Rates Tribunal). This consisted of three members appointed by the Minister of Transport, and its authorisation was necessary for schemes of charges in nationalised transport. Under the 1953 Act, schemes setting out only maximum charges were authorised, and such a scheme came into operation in 1957 on the railways. Traders could be charged less if the transport authorities wished. When increases were proposed, the Tribunal held hearings at which objections were raised from a miscellany of sources. It then issued its decision, which commonly made cuts in the proposals without giving reasons. The justification of this system lay in the monopoly power once held by transport services, particularly railways. In fact the railways have had to meet strong challenges in recent years from road services, whose charges were unregulated. Between 1948 and 1962 the Tribunal and other controls served to hamper competition in transport. The work of the Transport Tribunal has therefore been drastically reduced, and since 1962 it has dealt only with charges for passenger transport in London, and dock charges.

Other regulatory agencies with special relevance to nationalised industries include the Air Registration Board, which tests the airworthiness of new aircraft and the skill of maintenance engineers, and the Air Transport Licensing Board, which grants licences to operate regular air services and controls charges on internal routes.

The Mining Qualifications Board determines the technical compe-
tence of mine managers, and the relevant ministries, not the corporations, control the Mines Inspectorate and the Railways Inspectorate,
both concerned with safety questions.

These bodies are outside the main stream of accountability and
control. An attempt must now be made to put the general position in
perspective.

Theory and practice

Habitually, the problems of accountability and ministerial control
have been discussed in terms of too much or too little. The dangers of
too much supervision have been emphasised by the 'business efficiency' school of thought; the scandals of too little have been pointed
out by those who stressed the need for the application of constitutional and democratic principles. In fact, the issue of 'more' or 'less'
supervision has been misleading. The real need is to devise satisfactory *methods* of control and accountability, for there is general
agreement that detailed administration should be left alone and that
the boards should be answerable somehow for major policy. The
main method of accountability (the S.C.N.I.) has come near to a
solution of its side of the problem; the main method of ministerial
control (informal consultation) is less acceptable.

One of the greatest preoccupations of the boards has been their
fear of the adoption of restrictions appropriate to a public institution,
while at the same time measuring performance in the way used for
private enterprise. The sort of achievement that should be aimed at is
discussed in the next chapter. But it is relevant here to point out that
accountability for private industry is a very limited affair indeed.
The theory of the joint-stock public company is that its directors are
responsible to the shareholders, and answerable to them at annual and
other general meetings. In practice this procedure is almost always
a formality, and there exists great managerial freedom, highly
prized by leading businessmen. It is, of course, only the boards of
directors themselves who are so unhampered by supervision:
within the structure of large business organisations, systems of review
and control operate of necessity. But not having to explain past

actions became a custom of industrial management at the top, and this habitual freedom has made businessmen wary of different situations.

There is a sense in which private-enterprise companies may be held to be publicly accountable as well as accountable to their shareholders. They are required to publish certain information, and under certain circumstances the President of the Board of Trade can order an inquiry into a company's affairs. These arrangements are almost entirely concerned with the protection of investors and prospective investors. The conception of industrial management as a form of trusteeship, with responsibilities to employees, consumers, and the community, is widely held among businessmen today. But it has not been given any institutional form, and the public accountability of private enterprise remains rudimentary.

The question arises, of course, whether all techniques of accountability are as frustrating to initiative as businessmen usually have supposed. The notion of public accountability has normally been associated only with public ownership; but it is not, in the case of the nationalised industries, dependent on the spending of public money. If the principle is rather that of a fundamental responsibility to the community, then methods of accountability for large privately owned industrial concerns may be sought for.[19]

At all events, the disparity in public accountability has involved a disparity in public knowledge. If this leads to sounder public understanding, then it is to the advantage of the nationalised concerns; but if it leads to denigration and stress on their failings, then the absence of comparable sources of information about private industry can cause widespread resentment.

This chapter has shown how the two principles of Government control and public accountability have grown apart. The duty of public accountability, in the sense of giving explanations of how responsibilities are being carried out, does not necessarily imply control or further intervention. Only if it demonstrates serious deficiencies does it do that. It does provide a background of informed opinion, however, against which active control must operate.

The most serious result of the separation of accountability from control is constitutional. The influence of the Ministers on the industries is now much greater than they need acknowledge in the House of Commons, for they cannot readily be made responsible for private discussions. If a deficiency in public accountability remains, it is less with the industries themselves than with the Minister's power over the industries. The constitutional convention, that Ministers are responsible to Parliament for matters under their control, seems to be inadequately maintained in this field.

These developments — in accountability and in strong government influence — have led some critics to doubt the permanence of the public corporation as an independent institution. Professor A. H. Hanson, for example, states that '... one could write a history of public enterprise in this country since 1946 under the title of "The Decline and Fall of the Autonomous Public Corporation". Although its final chapters are still on the stocks, the general trend is unmistakable'.[20] Professor Hanson goes on to argue that similar trends exist in other countries, and that the need for the public corporation arose from misunderstandings about business efficiency. He suggests that it might be possible 'to preserve the form and something of the spirit of the public corporation and yet hold the nationalised industry entirely responsible to its Minister'.[21]

In the past there has been, in public controversy, an association between the case for maximum independence on the part of the boards and that for strict attention to commercial principles; on the other hand, those who favoured close control by Ministers also looked to 'public service' as a criterion of policy. In the next chapter these issues will be discussed, but it should be borne in mind here that abstracting the arguments about control and accountability brings in an element of artificiality. In assessing the viability of the theory of the public corporation, therefore, we should remember that much depends on what is taken to be the most important part of the theory.

In fact, the 'decline' of the public corporation has not been a decline in the corporate form for public trading activities: it has only been a decline in the autonomy of such bodies. The distinct

Government agency for business-type activities continues in most countries, and its widespread adoption in different parts of the world is one of the greatest tributes to its viability. In Britain atomic energy has been taken out of a Government department into an independent agency. The Post Office has moved since 1933 in the direction of greater commercial independence, and some people believe that it, or part of it, should become a public corporation. Thus the detachment of public industrial enterprise from the main structure of the Civil Service is hardly in question: separate staffing, the corporate form, and commercial accounting procedures have come to be practical necessities. The industrial undertakings are more than governmental bodies trading in a marginal way. Their conduct cannot be left to routine: it constantly needs policy decisions of an entrepreneurial character.

What is at stake, in fact, is not the public corporation *form* at all, but the degree of control and the nature of accountability.

It should be remembered that, as stated in Chapter 2, the detachment of the public corporation is only one feature of a much wider movement this century towards administrative independence. The causes of this are various, but they include the need for functional efficiency and the need to concentrate the attention of Parliament and Ministers on major issues. At all events, the general pressures for institutional variety in public bodies do not seem to have abated, and the position of the industrial public corporations cannot now be considered unusual or anomalous or experimental—there are too many institutions in similar circumstances.

The style of economic policy prevalent in the post-war years has depended on inducement and control at a remove; and in consequence, it has depended on a firm distinction between the (directly controlled) public sector, and a larger private sector (in need of persuasion). The White Paper of 1961 seems to indicate that special treatment of the nationalised industries has to some extent been withdrawn; if a more general planning system is successfully established, then discrimination may be further diminished.

There are some grounds for supposing that the idea of the public corporation, therefore, still has validity. It is certainly true that ministerial control in some cases is very close — the railways and the civil airlines are at present under strong policy guidance from their ministries. But this varies, as indeed the Ministers' concern with the private sector varies from industry to industry and from time to time. At least the public corporation offers scope for the relaxation and reimposition of Government control and parliamentary attention. It is not dead yet.

7   The Aims of
Nationalisation

The mere fact of ending private ownership in some of Britain's basic industries was undoubtedly a major political transformation. The new public corporations have had to cope with problems of organisation and control, reviewed in previous chapters. The fundamental issues now to be examined concern the objectives of public enterprise once it is securely established.

It was once a commonplace with both admirers and critics of capitalism that the object of private enterprises was to make as much profit as possible for their owners. In fact, the motives and behaviour of the controllers of private business are (and probably always were) more subtle and complex than this crude generalisation implies. Nevertheless, profit-seeking still provides a rationale for such concerns when they are in doubt about policy decisions; and it was on this assumption that ideas of competition in industry and the economists' theory of the firm were built.

No such simple rule exists for public enterprises, and the principles on which they are to be run are matters of deep controversy. The question that has to be answered, indeed, is that of the ultimate purpose of the activities of the nationalised industries: what, in the end, are their objectives?

The objects of private firms are decided by their directors and owners — whether they are wholly self-regarding, or whether they acknowledge a variety of responsibilities, is for them to decide, according to their lights. For nationalised concerns the issue runs deeper. It is a matter of public policy; of how the community as a whole should best be served. It is thus a matter of social or political philosophy. In the discussion that follows in this chapter much of the terminology is economic, but this should not disguise the fact that value judgments are necessary, and that moral principles underlie many of the issues in dispute. The way in which such considerations force themselves into the discussion—which arises from the needs of practical administrators in search of guidance— makes the topic almost as crucial for the political theorist as the question of public ownership itself.

The assumptions of the nationalisers

A beginning may be made by recalling the hopes and beliefs of those who were moved to end private ownership in these industries. What were their expectations?

They did not profess to have answers to all future problems, and they did not foresee many of them. Mostly they were persuaded that the weaknesses of the old system were so manifest that its replacement was the great issue. Other bridges—administrative, technical—might be crossed when they were reached. They had, however, a general background of economic ideas that were relevant.

First, the public enterprises would be non-profit-making. There would be no shareholders demanding satisfaction, and therefore the controllers of the concerns would not have to serve their interests. Nor were the industries to make profit for the purposes of the State. In the hands of a radical reformer like Joseph Chamberlain, municipal enterprise was used for revenue purposes, to reduce the rates. The break-even principle embodied in the Nationalisation Acts eschewed any such purposes.

Secondly, the nationalisers thought poorly of competition, certainly in the industries concerned. They recast the industries under unified management with monopolistic powers. The new corporations were regarded as vehicles for the administration of entire industries, rather than as enlarged firms.

Thirdly, the industries were enjoined to serve 'the public interest' in some sense. The full implications of this phrase were not clear, but it emphasised the rejection of private or sectional interests.

Fourthly, the industries would be subordinate to the Government and would be expected to co-operate fully with the Government's plans. In part, these plans would be prompted by Keynesian desires to maintain economic activity in the face of weak demand, but they would also be expected to help the location of industry and other political aims.

In the event, these views could serve only as the merest skeleton for policy guidance. At first there were urgent tasks to perform — reorganising industries, rehabilitating equipment after years of neglect, and overcoming serious shortages as peacetime demands asserted themselves. In these circumstances the question of the ideal policy seemed, to practical minds, academic and abstract.

Nevertheless, practical administrators were soon in need of guidance: about investment, about pricing, and about various priorities. Even before the post-war emergencies were over, it became necessary to form some ideas about the future development of nationalisation, and for this purpose it was clear that the motives (and prejudices) of the original nationalisers provided no adequate basis. Moreover, the Labour Government was replaced by a Conservative one in 1951, after only three or four years of nationalisation, and even where it did not denationalise, the new Government felt able to search for new styles of conduct.

The statutes

To some extent the views of the Labour Government that carried through the nationalisation process have been perpetuated because they were embodied in the statutes. They included rules about ministerial control, and they prescribed general duties relating to the public interest. The National Coal Board, for example, is charged with: '... making supplies of coal available, of such qualities and sizes, in such quantities and at such prices, as may seem to them best calculated to further the public interest in all respects, including the avoidance of any undue or unreasonable preference or advantage'.[1] Other Nationalisation Acts have similar passages. They also prescribe the break-even rule for finance — that revenue shall not be less than outgoings, taking one year with another — and so give some sketchy guidance for pricing policy.

K

The Transport Act of 1947 had prescribed a 'properly integrated' system as the goal of transport policy, but this was repealed by the Conservatives, just as they revised the structure of the electricity industry by legislation.

Pricing policy

The goods and services produced by nationalised industries are sold, in more or less free markets, to other industrial concerns or to final consumers. Prices are therefore subject to the forces of supply and demand, and the effects of variations in charges depend on conditions in the markets for the products. In Chapter 6 the great influence exercised by the Government on the prices charged by the public corporations was discussed. But how should these prices be decided?

In order to cover their costs as prescribed (and without aiming to maximise their profits), most of the nationalised industries began by basing their prices on the average of their costs. Critics, mainly economists, objected to this practice, and a long controversy about the merits of rival pricing rules took place. The argument of the critics favoured 'marginal costs' as the basis of prices, instead of average cost, and the controversy centred mainly on the coal industry. It is more costly to produce coal from some pits than others, and it was suggested that coal prices should be raised to the level of high-cost production (i.e. costs at the margin). This would encourage the efficient use of coal. It would also lead to a more accurate picture of the coal industry's claims to further development, since its higher prices would reflect the cost of producing additional coal. This case should be distinguished from another case for raising coal prices, which was based on the desirability of financing investment as far as possible from the Board's own resources.

The arguments about marginal- versus average-cost pricing flourished in academic as well as practical circles.[2] At first it was clear that marginal-cost prices would be substantially higher prices, and coal-consuming industries were reluctant to appreciate theoretical arguments leading to higher fuel costs. Moreover, the Government was engaged, in the 1950s, in a long struggle to hold down the general price level. In the Coal Board the concept of marginal cost seemed to have little relevance: in an extractive industry, additional production 'at the margin' is not available. Enlargement of output depends on a long-term programme of new investment. Again, the effects of marginal-cost pricing on coal industry finances would be extremely dramatic. Before 1957 there was a coal shortage, and marginal cost was well above average cost; this would have ensured large surpluses. The situation has now changed, and marginal cost is much lower than average cost (in 1964, about 40s. a ton compared with 87s. a ton). Prices at this level would involve very great losses.

The pricing policies of nationalised industries were also criticised for excessive uniformity. There was a tendency to charge flat rates for the whole country, irrespective of cost differences. Thus the Coal Board quoted prices for coal for domestic purposes delivered (to the merchants), and not pit-head prices—transport costs being averaged over the whole supply of this type of coal. The railways charged the same rate per mile for passengers at all times, though the rush-hour travellers made necessary much equipment that would not otherwise be required. Similarly, electricity consumed at peak hours —for which extra capacity is needed—was priced at the standard rate.

Over the years there have been considerable modifications to this practice. Differential tariffs have been introduced in the electricity industry; there is differential pricing in gas between districts; since 1956 railway charges for freight have taken account of commercial considerations; in 1961 the price of industrial coal produced in Scotland and the north-west (where costs are generally high) was raised above the standard level. Nevertheless, there is still a good deal of averaging in the nationalised industries. One reason for retaining it is administrative convenience, and another consumers' preference for seemingly equal treatment. But there are also possible grounds of public policy, and further consideration is given to the question later in the chapter.

What is the significance of these controversies for the aims of nationalisation? Broadly, those who advocated marginal-cost pricing and discrimination between consumers did so on economic grounds. They conceived the nationalised industries as very large firms, and expected them to be concerned with the maximisation of economic advantage for the community, through the proper allocation of resources. Some thought that imposing these principles on the public corporations was making the best of a bad job; others thought nationalisation could have positive advantages for the achievement of economic rationality. 'Nationalisation undoubtedly provides the ideal framework within which a proper integration of costs and prices could easily be arranged ... But the framework has not been used in this way.'[3]

In any case, the object of marginal pricing was to make the position of the nationalised industries dependent on consumers' preferences as these operated through the price mechanism. In Britain, democratic socialists and planners had always assumed that the freedom of the consumer would remain. Marginal-cost pricing would ensure, it was claimed, that consumers' choices were reflected in the relative prosperity (and future-output decisions) of industries. In principle the nationalised industries should be treated no differently from other industries, and their behaviour should be that which is expected, ideally, from competitive firms. The interests of the nation were best expressed through the market—a reformed market if necessary—and to allow nationalisation to distort market forces was to betray economic rationality.

The advocates of average-cost prices were not flatly opposed to these arguments: typically, they doubted only their practicability. But there was more than a hint of a different attitude to nationalisation in the remarks of some members of the Ridley committee:

> ... in their opinion the overriding principle is that coal is so important to the economy that it should be sold at the lowest price which is consistent with the National Coal Board's covering its costs. Indeed they assume that one advantage of the nationalisation of coal is to realise this principle ...[4]

In other words, a nationalised corporation should follow different principles from a privately owned one.

The disagreement about pricing policy was in fact the forerunner of a wider controversy about the behaviour appropriate to a nationalised industry.

The Herbert report and the commercial solution

Various implications of the report of the Herbert committee on electricity supply, published in 1956, have been discussed in previous chapters. Its most important contribution, however, lay in its thoroughgoing commendation of commercial principles: 'We state our view without any qualification that the governing factor in the minds of those running the Boards should be that it is their duty to run them as economic concerns and to make them pay.'[5]

The report carried the discussion well beyond the issue of pricing policy. It considered the role of the industry as a trading body, and declared at the outset that its efficiency was to be measured in strictly economic terms: success depended on meeting wants at the lowest possible cost. The committee dealt with all non-economic considerations that might affect policy by saying that they should be left to the decision of the Government.

In the report there was no shrinking from the consequences of its declared principles. The price of electricity was to be related as closely as possible to its costs, and those customers who caused the cost to rise should meet the increase – 'The first principle of tariff-making should be to secure that charges reflect the costs of supply.' Capital for the nationalised industries, said the report, would best be raised on the open market, without any special guarantees by the Government – though this should not apply to electricity if it did not also apply to the other nationalised industries.

Three examples of the committee's approach in more specific matters may be given. In its purchases of heavy electrical plant, the Central Authority had given precedence to British manufacturers, and had not sought tenders from abroad. The Herbert committee condemned this, and recommended that 'the Electricity Boards should seek the best and cheapest plant ... irrespective of origin.' Again, owing to the distances involved, the costs of

connecting new customers in rural areas are greater than in towns. The
boards should charge the customers for this, and the rate of progress
in making connections should be decided by the normal economic
and commercial tests. The retail trading of the boards through their
showrooms should be as vigorous and commercially progressive as
that of other concerns, and in hire purchase, for instance, they should
charge whatever rate the market would bear, despite their ability to
finance hire-purchase cheaply.[6]

The general philosophy of the Herbert report may be summed up
thus. The decisive criteria for judging an industry are economic;
other matters are peripheral. The nationalised industries should be
directed exclusively towards satisfying these economic standards;
other considerations should be imposed, if necessary, by the Government. The committee scarcely concealed its view that there would
be few occasions on which such interference was desirable; nor did
it conceal that private industry provided the model and exemplar
of what it proposed.

> We attach great importance therefore to the industry being run
> on business lines. It should have one duty and one duty alone:
> to supply electricity to those who will meet the costs of it and
> to do so at the lowest possible expenditure of resources consist-
> ent with the maintenance of employment standards at the level
> of the best private firms. Any deviation from this task should
> be undertaken only on precise instructions.[7]

The merits and the practicability of these unambiguous principles
must now be examined.

Difficulties of commercial principles

In Chapter 6 it was explained that Government control over the
nationalised industries had been greater than anticipated at the
outset. This in itself indicates that the freedom of action associated
with commercial principles has not been forthcoming. In spite of
the appeal that such principles had for Conservative politicians, it
was not found possible to apply very readily the doctrines of the
Herbert report to all the nationalised industries. The Government's

attitude was declared in a White Paper in 1961; but before this is described, the difficulties need to be explained.

(1) *Social costs.* Production always entails costs; in other words, some resources are used when goods or services are provided. For the use of resources —for labour, for capital, or for raw material —the producing organisation normally pays, and so meets its costs of production.

In practice, however, not all costs are charged to the producing organisation. Undesired effects of productive activity constitute costs, but sometimes the incidence of these effects is so widespread and indeterminate that no effective method of payment can be contrived. In other cases services are provided for the community at large, and producers do not pay for the use they make of them, except as general taxpayers. Examples of indeterminate incidence include pollution of the air by smoke and fumes, and inconvenience brought about by the operations of industry and transport —aircraft noise, for example. The provision of roads is an obvious example of a community service used by producers. The principle of both types is the same —costs of production are borne in some way by the community in general, not by the enterprise itself.

When an enterprise behaves solely in its own interest, it does not bother about these sorts of costs, because it does not have to pay for them directly. They are met in some way or other by the community as a whole, either by tax-financed provision or by leaving the general public to bear the losses they bring about. They are therefore part of 'social costs' (that is, the costs to society as a whole), but not of private or business costs.

In some cases, of course, better accounting and more ingenious methods of payment might enable some costs, now paid socially, to be brought home to those responsible. In the nature of things, however, full social costs are not easily chargeable.

From the operations of a nationalised industry, unpaid social costs may be incurred on a considerable scale, for they are large industries and often basic to the rest of the economy. What responsibility should the public corporations take for these costs?

The situation may best be explained through leading examples.

Aircraft noise has already been mentioned. Do the public airlines have responsibilities in this matter, beyond complying with regulations? Should they sponsor research? Should they operate quieter aircraft, if these are otherwise less efficient? It is clear that something should be done about this matter; what is not so clear is the distribution of responsibilities. Perhaps the Government should enforce stricter regulations. But without research and experience it is hard for them to judge what is practicable. If the corporations fly different aircraft, should they be compensated for any loss of revenue this brings about?

The extension of overhead electricity cables and pylons arouses perennial controversy. It costs ten or more times as much to put lines underground as it does to run them overhead; yet it is generally held that pylons and wires can do great damage to the beauty of landscape. How is this damage to be assessed, and at what point does it becomes worth while to put them underground? The problem is made particularly severe by the erection of a new 'supergrid' in the 1960s, and by the policy of building large, efficient power stations near the sources of fuel—that is, coalfields and oil refineries. It is cheaper to convey the electricity by cable to the big consuming areas (such as London) than to site the power stations there and transport the fuel. Nevertheless, the pylons bring about a social cost which, if it could be measured, might affect the true economics of the situation.

One of the best-known problems of social cost concerns the Scottish coalfield. (Social values and long-term considerations, discussed below, are also involved.) Many of the pits in Scotland operate at relatively high cost, and the National Coal Board is often urged to close them down. If this were done, there would be considerable unemployment and distress in mining towns and villages.[8] Much 'social capital'—housing, public services—would become redundant; and there would possibly arise a need for new social capital in places to which ex-miners moved. Should these costs, which fall on society as a whole, be estimated and taken into account by the Coal Board in deciding the future of the pits? Should the Board consider only the welfare of the industry, and leave social institutions to take care of the social consequences? Or are there other possibilities?

The greatest problems of social cost, however, are probably those concerning the transport system. In the first place, one form of transport (motor) uses facilities (roads) provided by the community. There is therefore a question of whether road users — especially particular types of road users — pay adequately, through taxation, for this provision. If they do not, then they have an artificial advantage over rival forms of transport (rail and air). Secondly, increased traffic on the roads brings about congestion, delay, and general loss of amenity for road users — that is, it causes social costs. Thirdly, when the retention of old forms of transport (such as the railway branch lines) or the building of new ones (such as motorways) is considered, the general advantage to a locality of good communications needs to be reckoned — many people benefit who never actually travel. There can be social gains as well as social losses.

It is in the transport field that the most elaborate attempts have been made to incorporate social costs into economic calculations. A technique of 'cost-benefit analysis' has been developed by which the full economic advantages and disadvantages to the community of a transport service can be measured.[9] It sometimes involves fairly bold estimation (e.g. in putting a money value on delays caused by congestion), but nevertheless provides a more reliable guide to the economics of transport services than do commercial accounts. Again, the question is whether nationalised transport itself should be guided by this type of analysis, or whether the analysis should be used by the Government merely to impose restraints.

(2) *Social and political values.* Important as they may be, social costs do not constitute the main 'social' problem for nationalisation. The fundamental issue is whether or not industrial policy is to be formulated in purely economic terms, and whether economic criteria alone provide a proper standard of judgment. Social costs are themselves an economic concept, and their consideration in policy-making serves only to establish a wider economic objective instead of a merely commercial one. There are, however, other matters

generally described as 'social' which cannot be dealt with in this way. These are social values such as freedom, equality, social justice and community spirit. We do not normally judge a society merely by its standard of living. We expect a variety of principles to be observed. Moreover, there is often agitation for reform and desire for improvement in directions which cannot be tested against the measuring rod of economic efficiency. Should such matters be taken into account in shaping the aims of nationalised industries?

Some examples may clarify the issue. In both employment and in customer relations there arise opportunities for racial or colour discrimination. Many people would expect the practice of a public corporation in such matters to be determined without reference to economic advantage. Publicly owned buses, for example, and British Railway hotels should not operate a colour bar, whatever effect there might be on their revenue. Again, when the public houses of Carlisle and near-by districts were nationalised, the objectives were not to maximise sales and profits: on the contrary, caution and restraint in sales were required at the time.

Scotland is a country with its own national identity. In order to sustain this identity within the United Kingdom, there is a need for social and economic standards to be comparable with those in England. If, therefore, the preservation of the quality of Scottish life is considered an end in itself worth pursuing, then industries may have to adapt their policies with this in mind. Similar considerations apply to Wales. It is also considered by many people that life in rural England should be sustained for its intrinsic social and aesthetic qualities. Transport and other services, particularly electricity, are therefore urged to make special efforts to meet rural needs.

A final example is provided by the employee's situation in modern industry. In spite of emergency provision through social services, most people are dependent on payment from work for their livelihood. Continuous and secure employment has great importance for the maintenance of the tenor of individual and family life, therefore, beyond its economic function as an exchange of purchasing power for current labour services. It may be held, consequently, that employment should be maintained wherever possible, and that individual enterprises have social obligations in this matter, since they are the direct providers of employment and actively demand the services of employees most of the time.

In short, these examples derive from conceptions of 'society' and 'social' as something wider, more comprehensive, and in some ways embodying higher values than 'economy' and 'economic'. In consequence, the economic organisation should, it is claimed, adapt the requirements of its own maximum efficiency to meet the greater human needs described as 'social'.

There is also a political order, which in turn has requirements for successful functioning. To meet them an industrial enterprise might be expected, for example, to accept collective bargaining and joint consultation, and to eschew personal and partisan discrimination, whether or not these were to its commercial advantage. The system of public accountability described in the last chapter can be justified as a contribution to the *political* well-being of the nation, irrespective of its effect on the efficiency of the nationalised industries.

The counter-arguments to these views do not deny that 'social' and 'political' values are often of great importance, though it can be suggested that they are used merely as forms of resistance to change.[10] What is disputed is the responsibility for taking care of such values. All social activity, including economic activity, has side effects and long-run consequences, many of which cannot be foreseen. It is not reasonable, it is argued, to expect industrial managers to make assessments of these matters. Particular institutions should concentrate on doing their own jobs well, and for nationalised industries this means concentrating on economic efficiency. If in some cases there is a pressing need to look to social or political matters, then this should be done by those responsible, presumably the Government itself. Where action is considered necessary, it should be imposed by external authority. This solution – leaving non-commercial matters to the Government – recurs throughout this chapter. Its adoption might mean the clarification of responsibilities, but it is probably too much to hope that there would be any clear distinction between social values and the other factors – social costs, national

economy, and the long term—discussed in this section. Yet the
existence of this category is perhaps the most fundamental point
to grasp about the formulation of policy objectives—because it is
the most difficult to assimilate to any formula.

(3) *The national economy*. The nationalised industries are adjured
by statute to pay attention to 'the public interest'. This constitutes
an obligation to work for something more than the good of themselves or any other limited group or section of the community.
When the extent and causes of ministerial intervention were set out
in Chapter 6, the key role of ideas about the national interest was
apparent, the most important notion being that of central direction
of the economy in order to maintain full employment, to check
inflation, and to promote growth. This implies that the policies of
the nationalised industries were to be subordinated to more general
ends. The subordination has had two aspects.

In the first place, the formulation of high policy for the industries
should take place with the broad economic prospects for the nation
in the forefront. In other words, there should be an attempt to foresee
a role for the industry in the economy. The success of a particular
nationalised industry should be achieved in such a way that it har-
monises with other industrial developments. Ultimately, it is the
success of the whole economy that is aimed at, and the success of a
nationalised industry is measured by its contribution to the total
situation.

Secondly, nationalised industries are expected to co-operate to the
full in the current economic policies of the Government of the
day. Wages, prices and investment programmes have all had to be
adapted to comply with emergency programmes devised by the
Government to meet critical economic situations. The story of the
attempts by the Government to direct the economy in the 1950s and
the means used to promote stability and progress are too complex
to rehearse here.[11] The programmes were applied, of course, over
the whole economy and not just in the public sector. But the
political and administrative power of the Government ensured that
such measures were not neglected or evaded by the public corporations; indeed, there was a feeling that unless the nationalised indus-

tries provided a good example, other enterprises could scarcely be expected to comply.

An example of how the policy of a nationalised industry was expected to fit in with national needs was given by Sir James Bowman, chairman of the National Coal Board, in 1957. The prices obtainable for British coal in Europe were much higher than those on the home market, yet only limited exports were allowed by the Government, in view of the need for adequate fuel supplies in Britain.[12] From the point of view of the economy as a whole, this might have been reasonable, but it was clearly not in the interest of the Coal Board's finances.

It must be emphasised that the national interest in these matters is conceived in economic terms. Social and political values are not necessarily at stake here. The difficulty for the 'commercial solution' is, rather, that the nationalised industries have been expected to sacrifice their own immediate financial advantage to *wider* economic purposes. Clearly, non-commercial factors discussed under other headings may also be national in scope.

(4) *The long term.* There is a further type of public interest which has affected nationalisation policies but which is difficult to classify. Considerations of this type are not commercial, because they could not enter into the ordinary calculations or accounts of the corporations. They may, however, be at least partly economic in character, if guesses and hopes about *future* material welfare can be regarded as economic. Since the benefit will mainly accrue, if at all, to later generations, it may perhaps be right to regard attention to them as being fundamentally of a moral or ideological character.

The atomic energy programme for civil purposes is perhaps the most striking example. It is largely a research and development activity, and so far none of the nuclear power stations that have resulted have been able to produce electricity as cheaply as modern conventional stations. Nevertheless, the programme is persisted with, and in 1965 it appeared that at last a new type of advanced gas-cooled reactor was being developed that would make nuclear generation economically worth while. There also appears to be in the background a belief in the need to develop nuclear technology in

Britain as an essential scientific skill; to neglect it would endanger the country's future intellectual, if not economic, independence.

This is, of course, only one aspect of the question of the security of future fuel supplies. The demand for productive energy in the world has been rising rapidly and seems likely to continue to do so. The costs and availability of supplies for Britain from abroad must always be relatively uncertain, in face of this rising world demand, and it is therefore argued that prudence dictates special care of indigenous production, mainly the coal industry. Mining skills, technology, and capital equipment are all highly specific; closed pits cannot be reopened like factories; and the development of new mines is expensive and slow. The long-term needs of Britain for secure energy supplies therefore imply some protection for the coal industry against short-run fluctuations in market forces. At present the import of coal from abroad is not authorised, and since 1961 there has been a tax on fuel oil which protects coal in some uses.

The rehabilitation of the railways affords a further example. Market forces allowed to operate commercially would not have sustained the railways as a going concern, let alone provided capital for modernisation. Yet future transport needs are likely to be such that an efficient railway system will be essential, and investment now by the Government can be justified by future economic and social requirements.

The situation of the airlines also contains elements that may be regarded as matters of long-term faith, though national prestige is said to be involved as well. At least up to 1964, B.O.A.C. flew certain international routes, subsidised some other connected airlines, and ordered British-made aircraft to an extent which could be regarded as commercially prudent only on the most optimistic calculation of future developments. In July 1964 the Minister of Aviation, Mr Julian Amery, insisted that B.O.A.C. take twenty British VC-10 aircraft, though the chairman, Sir Giles Guthrie, would have preferred to cancel the orders and buy American aircraft instead. This helped the British aircraft construction industry, whose continued survival was thought to be in the long-term national interest.

When the supply of capital is involved in these problems, it may be said that private investors are capable of taking a long-term view, and that their judgments of future national needs (and hence of the future prospects of the industries) are likely to be as reliable as those of the Government. The sums involved are often very large, however; and the long term may be very long indeed. The answer of the capital market, in fact, is not in doubt: the funds would not be available. In these circumstances the Government has to decide for itself whether the future, as it sees it, justifies special treatment for the industries.

Cross-subsidisation

These four types of difficulties show that the principle of commercial operation cannot be applied easily and without qualification. Before there can be any general assessment of the argument, however, a further issue must be broached—that of cross-subsidisation and subsidies in general. If there are, for argument's sake, to be activities of public corporations that do not pay for themselves, how are they to be sustained? How is the extra finance to be provided?

The essential principle of cross-subsidisation may be explained briefly. Production involves costs, and since it is the consumer who gets the benefit of the production, it seems appropriate that the producing organisation should look to him to meet the full costs of what he receives. If this does not happen, there is a likelihood of misdirection of production, for strong demand will arise from people who are being undercharged. Moreover, if the demand from consumers is not a fair reflection of their wants, then the controllers of industry will make distorted decisions when planning future production. In any case, the payment of artificially low prices by one set of consumers means that others are paying unnecessarily high prices; that is, a subsidy is being paid. If this process occurs within the range of a single organisation, it constitutes a concealed or cross-subsidy.

In a sense, cross-subsidies are unavoidable in business operations. It is impossible to cost every sale; and in any case prices must be announced in advance, before all costs can be known. In practice the

problem is concerned with charges made for similar types of products or ranges of goods, or to similar classes of customers. Should
cross-subsidisation occur, that is to say, even though it may be
administratively practicable to avoid it?

There are many instances of this problem in the nationalised
industries. The Electricity Act of 1947 instructed the new boards
to 'promote the simplification and standardisation of methods of
charge'. This principle invited cross-subsidisation, for a simple tariff
might not reflect the different costs involved in supplying different
types of customer (e.g. industrial, commercial, and domestic) at
different times of day (peak hours and off-peak). Similarly, on the
railways fares are standardised, though costs on different routes, at
different seasons and at different times may vary greatly. The
problem appears more acutely where really high-cost supplies are
involved, and where easily reckoned losses are incurred. Some of the
problems have already been mentioned, such as the high-cost coal
mined in Scotland, the expensive rail services on branch lines, some
air routes, and rural electrification. Normal or 'standard' charges
in these cases mean (if there is no external subsidy and the board
concerned is not making a loss) that other customers are paying
more than they need. Therefore, besides the question of actually
maintaining these high-cost services, for social or national reasons,
there arises the question of whether the other customers of the boards
are the appropriate source of funds for the purpose. This constitutes
the essence of the cross-subsidisation issue.

Cross-subsidisation may take more subtle forms, though the
issue is the same in principle. Certain railway or airline routes may
pay very well, but no reduction in charge is made, because the
corporation wants to build up its profits or its reserves, or check its
losses. Revenue from profitable services may in practice enable a
corporation to offer keen prices where it faces sharp competition
or wishes to make a special effort. The Coal Board, for instance,
tries to keep down the price of anthracite, though it is expensive to
produce, in order to compete in the market for domestic central
heating. A distinction may perhaps be made between cross-subsidisation that occurs because the producing organisation discriminates

in the allocation of overhead costs (some activities not paying their fair share); and cross-subsidisation in which some activities do not meet even their direct costs. These latter forms are usually enforced, by moral or administrative pressure, or by legal obligation.

The successful practice of cross-subsidisation depends on the strength of the sellers in certain directions, which are used to sustain the weaker lines. Usually a degree of monopoly is necessary. Nationalised industries have statutory rights which give them the necessary monopoly advantages in many fields, and hence a measure of cross-subsidisation is available to them.

The need to cross-subsidise can constitute a burden, however. Even the legal monopolies of the public corporations do not protect them against all types of competition—other types of products or forms of services may be substituted for the ones they provide. Hence to compel nationalised industries to pay cross-subsidies may hamper their competitiveness in lines where they should be strongest. If main-line railway transport, for example, has to be profitable enough to carry non-paying lines, then it may itself have unnecessary difficulty in competing with road vehicles or internal airlines. Nor, in such a case, would the fares put before the prospective traveller reflect the true costs of the alternatives.

For these reasons cross-subsidies are not particularly popular within the nationalised industries. Nevertheless they continue to exist, and there are reasons that impel the corporations to maintain them.

There is, of course, no case for eliminating cross-subsidies where the accounting or administrative expenses of doing so nullify the gains. This factor can be very important, for the maintenance of public goodwill may be involved. There may be an element of social cost if the methods of charging create time-consuming trouble and expense for the customers.

Cross-subsidies are also maintained for the purpose already reiterated—to meet 'social' needs, and to keep up productive units or markets that may be viable in the future, but which could not easily be restarted if stopped. Among these non-paying activities may also be included 'pioneering' enterprises. New air routes, for example, or new types of fuel on the home market, may not pay at first, especially if heavy capital or development costs are included. If these are regarded as promotional activities, the losses can be treated as capital expenditure. But if the ventures are paid for out of current revenue, this amounts to a cross-subsidy.

Cross-subsidisation may exist on the initiative of the public corporation itself, or by its reluctance to remove the more subtle forms of it. It may also exist at the instigation of the Government. The willingness of the Government to encourage cross-subsidisation in particular cases may enable the industry to appeal for protection of one sort or another. If cross-subsidisation is to succeed, then monopoly advantages elsewhere may be necessary; and if the whole policy is agreed on with the Government, then governmental powers may be used in its support. Thus if the Government agrees to maintain coal working in central Scotland, then some protection to the coal industry may be appropriate.

The alternative to cross-subsidies is, of course, open subsidies. The Government may choose to sustain particular activities or a level of general activities from its own funds, as it has done for the railways. If capital projects are involved, it may lend money on favourable terms.

The open subsidy has great advantages. It makes clear to all concerned what is happening. The finances of the public corporations are not put at a disadvantage. Morally it seems proper that an activity wanted by the Government (as the agent of the community) should be paid for by the Government (through taxes on the whole community). Nevertheless, there are also disadvantages. Methods of calculating appropriate subsidies are not entirely satisfactory. Regular payment of fixed amounts lessens the incentive to reduce costs, and this lack of cost-consciousness may spread to other activities of the corporation. The attitude may arise that all non-paying activities deserve subsidy. Nor may it be easy for a Government to find the money—there is, after all, strong popular hostility to taxation. It has been suggested, for example, that local authorities might subsidise local branch railways. Yet any further burden on the rates would be politically difficult and socially unfair.

Cross-subsidisation seems likely, with some effort, to be diminished. But it is unlikely to be abolished. It does not discourage cost-consciousness quite so much as do regular outside subsidies, and it sometimes provides a means of relatively painless finance for necessary services.

The White Paper of 1961

An attempt has been made by the Government to formulate official doctrines about some of the questions raised in this chapter. The drafting of the statement no doubt helped the Government to clarify its views and in any case the public and the nationalised industries themselves were entitled to know the Government's attitude.

The White Paper, *The Financial and Economic Obligations of the Nationalised Industries*,[13] consists mainly of a review of the industries in financial terms. It prescribes a new framework in which they are to work:

(*a*) The obligation to meet costs 'taking one year with another' was made more precise — surpluses were to cover deficits over a five-year period, if possible. Moreover, revenue should include provision for replacement of assets as they become worn out or obsolete, and for further capital development. After discussion, each industry would be set a target for the five-year period (subject to review each year), which would indicate how much revenue, beyond its bare running costs, it should try to earn.

(*b*) The existing practices in relation to investment and borrowing were endorsed — that is to say, forward plans would be examined by the Ministries, and special attention would be given to those expected to yield a low return.

(*c*) These proposals meant that the industries would have to try to increase their net revenue. In the past many of them had made losses even over five-year periods; and they had not provided much of their investment funds. The main way to secure the increased revenue would be to reduce costs. But the White Paper recognised that the industries must be given freedom to alter their prices — in practice to raise them—in order to meet the prescribed financial standards.

(*d*) Price rises were one of the matters discussed in Chapter 6; it was noted that Ministers had considerably restricted the industries' freedom of action. The White Paper stated that the arrangements for discussing prices would continue, but that public statements might be made if a board's proposals were altered (see p. 120).

(*e*) The Government accepted the view that commercial performance might be hampered by non-commercial activities. It did not propose that all these should be abandoned. Nor did it propose to provide subsidies from its own finances. The solution announced was to take these non-commercial activities into the reckoning when calculating the five-year target:

> These activities will, so far as practicable, have been taken into account in fixing the financial standard for each undertaking. To the extent that commercially unprofitable activities are subsequently imposed from outside, a Board would be entitled to ask for an adjustment of its financial objectives.[14]

In the next two years, financial objectives were agreed on these lines with the various boards. They vary from industry to industry and are expressed in different ways, but they represent generally a return of between six and eight per cent on the value of their assets (calculated after allowing for depreciation). In calculating the five-year objectives the special character and prospects of each industry are taken into account. The White Paper acknowledges the 'public utility' nature of many of the industries, and does not expect from them the same performance as from other industries. They are different, that is to say, because they are basic industries rather than manufacturing concerns, not because they are nationalised. The railways have special financial arrangements, already described, and are excluded from this framework for the time being.

In general, the White Paper was regarded as a step towards commercial standards. Certainly the new five-year formulae are more realistic than the statutory 'one year with another' doctrine; and the greater precision means that both the industries and the Government can manoeuvre only within strict limits in their attitude to prices. This pro-commercial tendency of the White Paper is openly declared at the beginning: '. . . They are not . . . to be regarded as social services absolved from economic and commercial justification.'[15] However, in the last paragraph there is a different emphasis:

> The nationalised industries are from their size and nature bound to play a major role in the economic life of the country. They cannot, however, be regarded only as very large commercial concerns which may be judged mainly on their commercial results: all have, although in varying degrees, wider obligations than commercial concerns in the private sector. The object of these proposals is to find for each industry or Board a reasonable balance between these two concepts.

There is of course no direct contradiction between this passage and earlier parts of the White Paper. Nevertheless, this is not the language of the Herbert report. Once 'wider obligations' are stipulated, the criteria of policy-making must lose their economic simplicity.

Some comments may be appropriate. It is difficult to see how the five-year targets can be used as tests of efficiency, even though the White Paper treats failure to reach the objectives as 'inadequate performance'.[16] The targets are determined by administrators, after negotiation with the boards, and determined in advance. They are, therefore, in a sense predictions—not predictions of what will happen, but predictions that the objectives will be reasonable. As things turn out, the targets may be very difficult or very easy to achieve. Failure to achieve the required result may illustrate the fallibility of the Ministry's prediction about future circumstances just as much as the weakness of the industry. The provision for annual review seems to recognise this. In any case, the board was appointed by the Minister, and, even on the narrowest interpretation of his functions, he must carry responsibility before Parliament for choosing competent board members.

It seems, therefore, that the five-year targets should be regarded as essential working rules for the industries, on which they can base policy decisions, rather than as objective tests for measuring the quality of their performance.

In sum, the White Paper proposed a new economic self-reliance for the industries. Their policies on prices were no longer to be subordinated to anti-inflationary needs, to public pressure, or to other non-commercial considerations. The White Paper stressed that this would end any excess demand brought about by low prices, or over-investment occasioned by the excessive demand.

It has been argued, in fact, that the low-price (and loss-making) period in the nationalised industries brought considerable advantages to industrial consumers, who were getting products and services below cost. Between 1949 and 1958, it has been suggested, a 'subsidy' averaging £100 million a year was paid out by the nationalised industries to their customer industries—that is, they were under-charged by that amount.[17] It should also be remembered, however, that the undercharging brought financial weakness which meant that investment funds had to be obtained, through the Government, from the rest of the community. This borrowing process, of course, carried a burden of interest payments not necessary with self-finance.

The new self-reliance of the nationalised industries is of course not absolute. It promises some relaxation of the subordination to 'national economy' considerations, but the influence of social costs, social values, and long-term beliefs can still weigh heavily in the balance of policy-making. The White Paper gave a new degree of flexibility, but it is only a degree, and the need to agree special rates of return, and so on, merely emphasises the strong position of the Ministers.

Monopolies and frontiers

A group of issues adjacent to the main lines of discussion must now be described.

There has been a general tradition that publicly owned enterprises are conducted as monopolies. In part this was because it was believed

that competition could not work without the profit motive; partly
because it was thought that fair competition between privately
owned and publicly owned concerns would be difficult to contrive;
and partly because the industries concerned were 'natural' monopolies. Indeed, the existence of situations where monopoly was
virtually inevitable, such as the supply of gas, provided a strong
argument for public ownership in these cases.

When industries were nationalised in 1946–9 the monopoly
rights of the public corporations were set out in the Acts, and so
made legally enforceable.[18] Not only were existing enterprises
taken over, that is to say, but new ventures by private concerns into
the industries, as defined, were forbidden. In practice, however, the
situation is complicated. There is no doubt that the legal security
of the public corporations within defined limits gives them great
advantages. The need to meet certain types of competition, however, has been for many of them their most urgent problem. How
does this arise?

It is a very common mistake, particularly in relation to public
enterprise, to talk about monopoly in terms of the structure of
industry. The important arena is the market, and it is the situation
among suppliers to the same market (i.e. among those trying to meet
the same sort of demand) that is really significant. Thus the National
Coal Board undoubtedly has a monopoly of coal production (apart
from small mines). For many purposes, however, there are rival
fuels to coal—in the markets for domestic heating and electricity
generation, for example, it has to face stiff competition from fuel
oil. The legal monopolies of public corporations provide varying
degrees of protection, according to the availability of substitutes.
The most effective monopoly at present among the nationalised
industries probably lies with the use of electricity for lighting purposes.[19] In heating and other fuel uses there is a strongly competitive situation, and in most sectors of transport one form can be
substituted for another. There is also the possibility, in principle, of
imports, but there can be little challenge to the present nationalised
industries from foreign competitors in exactly the same lines.

In recent years the Government has refused permission for the import of coal, though before 1957 the Coal Board itself imported some from the United States and resold it at British prices —that is, at a loss. B.O.A.C. must, of course, from the nature of its routes, meet constant competition from foreign airlines.

In the 1950s the traditional policy of monopoly operation for public enterprise was considerably modified. The Conservative Government was at the time pursuing a policy of freedom from control and the elimination of monopolistic agreements in private industry. It was natural to accompany this by encouraging competition in public enterprise. Except for the break-up of the original British Transport Commission, the structure of nationalisation was not much changed. By one means or another, however, the various industries were put into positions where they were more and more dependent on market situations and had to face competition from a variety of sources. During this period, too, opinion in the Labour Party became more favourable to competition, certainly in private industry, and under certain conditions in public enterprise. The 'competition' that was advocated and that emerged did not of course amount to anything like full competition in the economist's sense. Sometimes it was little more than a spirit of emulation or rivalry between different Areas or Regions, for example. In other cases it meant that privately owned concerns would be allowed a share of the market, as with independent airlines on internal routes. It was not essential for new private enterprises, or indeed any private enterprise, to be involved. Competition can lie between various public corporations just as it does between private firms. There is no motivation towards profit maximisation, but experience shows that administrative and psychological incentives are sufficient to make such competition an effective driving force. There is at present sharp competition in domestic heating between the Coal Board and the electricity and gas authorities (as well as the oil companies); and there is competition between British Railways, British Road Services, the Transport Holding Company, and British European Airways in meeting particular demands.

The question of 'frontiers' is closely associated with that of monopoly. Just as the statutes protect the public corporations from competition within their range of operations, so they often debar the corporations from activities outside that range. In some cases the Acts contain explicit prohibitions of particular activities; in other cases the limitations arise from discouragement by the Government or the restraint of the corporations themselves.

These limits put the corporations at several disadvantages. In the first place, the real limits of an 'industry' must always be vague, and strict rules may prevent natural expansion into ancillary activities. In fact, the public corporations acquired a number of ancillary and miscellaneous businesses in the process of nationalisation—such as brickworks, coking plant and farms by the Coal Board, and bus companies and travel agencies by nationalised transport concerns. For many years there were no extensions of this type of activity, but eventually some joint ventures with private enterprise were set up —for instance, B.O.A.C. has a link with Cunard, and the Coal Board has joined with J. H. Sankey & Son, builders' merchants, in marketing solid fuel appliances. Secondly, the establishment of large public corporations is both the effect and cause of the growth of 'countervailing' organisations—large firms, combines, and trade associations which bargain with the corporations as suppliers and customers. The strict frontier injects an element of artificiality and rigidity into this process. Neither can advance into the territory of the other; and in particular the public corporations could not, before 1965, undertake manufacturing or distributive activities which they might have found advantageous. Thus the Central Electricity Generating Board does not produce its own generating plant, nor do the Area Boards of gas and electricity manufacture appliances, though they distribute them. The Coal Board does not manufacture mining machinery, and it has not extended its interest in the merchanting of coal to domestic consumers beyond the three per cent of the trade that it inherited on nationalisation. The railways, however, have traditionally manufactured much of their own equipment, including rolling stock, in railway workshops. They have also bought from a sizeable private-enterprise industry. The allocation of orders between the two has always been a problem. In 1962 a plan for the rationalisation of railway workshops was set up, reducing the number of main works from twenty-eight to sixteen. Moreover, the workshops were to compete with outside firms for construction contracts offered by British Railways themselves. On the other hand, railway workshops did not compete for contracts offered by concerns other than British Railways which they might have secured. In 1964 and 1965 the Labour Government removed the restrictions, and railway workshops were permitted to obtain work from other customers, private and foreign, besides British Railways. It is only in recent years that British Railways have pursued an active policy to make the best and most profitable use (for non-railway purposes) of the many valuable sites that they own. Until 1965, B.O.A.C. was debarred from competing for contracts with the Service ministries for carrying troops to and from overseas stations.

There have been also specific restraints on production for export. Both the 1947 Electricity Act and the 1948 Gas Act prohibited manufacture for export, even in circumstances where production of equipment for use by the boards themselves is allowed.[20] In 1965 legislation to ease these restrictions was foreshadowed.[21]

Finally, there is the question of general diversification. One of the courses open to a private-enterprise concern is to widen its interests, either by setting up new production itself or by combining with an existing firm. Nationalised industries have not been in the habit of developing in this way. For activities closely allied to those of the main enterprise there could be obvious advantages in integration. But also by establishing itself in relatively disparate fields, a business can insure itself against difficulties, both temporary and long-term, in its original line. Such flexibility has not been generally available to the nationalised industries. The 1965 White Paper on *Steel Nationalisation*, however, emphasised that the proposed National Steel Corporation would acquire firms with interests in such things as structural engineering, bridge-building and wire manufacture; and moreover, that the Corporation would be able to further diversify its activities when this appeared commercially advantageous.[22]

The existence of the 'frontier' implies a crude balance of disadvantages between the public corporations and private business. The

limitation on diversification, however, seemed to give private
industry the best of the bargain. Private industry could not enter the
cage that protected nationalised concerns, but the public corporations were deprived of the greater scope outside.

It is not difficult to see how these matters affect the aims of
nationalised industries. From the point of view of commercial
success, the easiest situation is provided by effective monopoly;
second best would be complete freedom of manoeuvre on the
frontier. Few governments are likely to countenance either of these
extremes, and the corporations must expect to face some competition
and to put up with some limitations on the scope of their activities.
Within this range of practical possibility, various controversies
proceed, usually on familiar lines.

Thus it may well be argued that competition between public and
private enterprise is a good thing. But is the competition fair?
Public enterprise may feel that the flexibility of its rivals, and their
freedom to neglect social responsibilities, gives them unfair advantages. It is alleged that private firms operating on the fringes of
nationalised industries do not undertake costly research or training
programmes, and often fail to provide relatively unremunerative
'staple' services, confining their competitive efforts to the more
lucrative parts of the trade. On the other hand, some private firms
might complain that the ancillary and competitive activities of the
public corporations are aided and supported by the statutory-
monopoly activities, which provide technical and management
skills, if not actual cross-subsidies; and, moreover, there is less need
for the public enterprise to make a regular profit.[23]

Another field of controversy concerns competition among the
nationalised industries themselves. There are some who suggest
that the co-ordination and integration natural within each corporation should be extended over the whole of public industry. Wide
co-operation was indeed proposed under the original Transport Act
of 1947. When the Ridley committee reported in 1952 on national
fuel policies, however, it recommended that consumers should be
left to choose between competing services.[24] In 1959, moreover, the
Weir committee reported on co-operation between electricity and

gas boards, and found there was no substantial advantage to be got
from their co-operation in meter reading, collection of accounts,
service centres and showrooms, advertising, or the breaking up of
streets.[25] In fact the public corporations have always behaved commercially towards one another, and in the fuel and power industries
there now seems to be wide agreement that this is the right policy.
In transport the high social costs involved suggest that more integration may be possible.

The relevance of these issues to the question of objectives lies
therefore in the environment that monopoly or competition provides. If the corporations are to sustain prescribed standards of performance, then they must be concerned about the circumstances in
which they operate. Social and political obligations are well-known
factors affecting performance. The degree of monopoly and the
room for manoeuvre on industrial frontiers are less often considered,
but are no less important. There can be little doubt that, by encouraging competition without granting additional scope on the frontiers,
recent Conservative Governments have, on balance, made life harder
for the boards. The succeeding Labour Government has given the
corporations greater opportunities. Which policy contributes to
general economic efficiency is a matter of political dispute. For this
chapter, however, the point is that the competitive environment of
a public trading enterprise is a vital consideration in determining
its commercial, social and political objectives.

A reassessment

It is now possible to attempt a summary and an evaluation of the
various arguments set out in this chapter. It is convenient to begin
by reiterating the case for a commercial approach.

Its main administrative appeal lies in its clarity. It provides in
most cases an unmistakable criterion by which to test the success
of a policy. Moreover, it is a criterion which can be used to compare
dissimilar activities, and which can be understood (and enforced)
throughout the administrative structure of large organisations. The
strictly commercial approach also has claims to be grounded in
economic logic. The plain facts of economic life must eventually be

faced, and if only projects that pay are taken up, then the facts will be faced sooner rather than later. The demand of consumers through the market is, moreover, a plain fact, and hence it is a surer basis for policy than the views of politicians and managers about social needs, the national interest, or future developments.

Even if commercial standards cannot be applied without exception, the commercial principle does provide a practicable distinction between the responsibilities of the corporations, which should be entirely commercial, and those of the Government, which may be based on other considerations. This was the view of the Herbert committee, and a similar attitude has been repeatedly taken up by the Select Committee on Nationalised Industries.

Most of the difficulties and objections to the rigorous application of commercial principles have already been rehearsed. It may be that its clarity — arising from its simplicity — is a reason for suspecting its validity, as well as being an administrative merit. The old laissez-faire doctrines also had the merit of simplicity, but this was eventually a cause of their downfall: they did not meet the complexity of human needs. As the White Paper insists, the nationalised industries are not social services. But does it follow that there can only be two styles of organisation — the social service, totally financed by the Government, and the commercial enterprise, with no support whatsoever? In fact, charges are made for some social services. It may also be convenient to meet the objectives of social policy, once they are decided, by subsidies, cross-subsidies, or measures of protection; and the nationalised industries have no claim to stand aside from this process.

The most popular form of the 'commercial solution' is undoubtedly the modified doctrine whereby non-commercial activity is allowed, even welcomed, so long as it takes place at the behest of the Government. A great deal turns on the practicability and effectiveness of this doctrine. The Government certainly has general responsibility for all aspects of national welfare and should be in a position to give proper weight to social and political factors. There are some things which can be done *only* by the Government, such as determining an industry's role in a national plan, or providing a degree of protection. In any case, the British constitutional system gives the Government of the day the power to impose its will, and it would be difficult for a Government to avoid final responsibility for industrial affairs.

Yet it may be doubted if this doctrine provides a real answer to the problem. Social and political considerations are not occasional occurrences: they pervade the whole conduct of industry. More-over, the points at which they arise are not always national in scope: they are often local or individual. National rulings about social standards need to be interpreted, therefore, by managers well down the industrial hierarchy. To declare a doctrine of 'commercial opera-tion only' is to pre-empt the social decisions of these managers. Again, the decisions of the Government on social matters cannot fail to be influenced by the attitudes of the chairmen of the public corporations. Ministers are under pressure from the public and their parties, but they will not be helped to wise decisions if they are confronted by the industries' universal hostility to all social claims.

The situation therefore calls at least for understanding and discrimination about social matters by the management of the industries themselves. Industrial decisions which involve social and political values—such as freedom, equality and accountability—will be better taken if the managers of nationalised industries par-ticipate in them, and if they are able to take a constructive attitude which recognises the plurality of values usually prevalent in British society. Their examination of such issues will be improved, more-over, if they have some understanding of the distinctions between the types of factor involved.

Can anything be said, in a more positive way, about the ends that the industrial public corporations should pursue?

There is no dispute, of course, that the *main* purposes of a national-ised industry must be economic, even though these may be over-ridden at times. It is worth while, therefore, trying to define the main economic purpose more clearly.

Economic activity is concerned with the production of real wealth —goods and services. From the community's point of view, a successful economic project is one that produces a large difference between the value of what goes in (raw materials, fuel, depreciation of capital) and the value of the output. This difference (the economist's 'value-added') provides the income of labour and that of capital.

Now, the motives of the controllers of free-enterprise firms are complex, and the principles guiding their decisions have achieved some sophistication. The whole force of their legal obligations, however, lies in satisfying their shareholders. In the past this has been regarded as a sufficient explanation of their behaviour. There are now views that stress the multiple purposes of all enterprises. For private enterprise, however, the absence of any substantial system of public accountability means that any modifications of objective, economic or otherwise, must arise from within.

A nationalised industry has no built-in motives of this sort. Its economic purposes can only be understood as part of a wider operation – the maximisation of value-added for the community. It will need some guidance, from national planners or market forces, on the scale of its contribution. It may be prudent for it to make some profit, as part of its investment programme. But the general measure of its economic success must lie in the value it adds to the community's goods and services, and not merely in the part of that addition which appears as a surplus or is used for the remuneration of capital-providers. Indeed, since some of this value may be distributed, not to labour or capital, but to consumers in the form of lower prices, its size may not be calculable at all.[26]

An economic criterion for determining the policies of nationalised industries has been put forward by Mr Christopher Foster in *The Transport Problem*.[27] He argues that an attempt to provide the greatest benefit for everybody (maximum social surplus) by the operations of an enterprise would be impractical: the necessary calculations could not be made. But he suggests an interesting alternative to a criterion of profit maximisation: a public enterprise could aim to maximise the 'surplus' available to its consumers – that is, it could aim to provide as great a difference as possible between the value to them of the goods, and the costs they have to meet, including provision for investment. To do this, an enterprise should base all its prices on the average cost of producing the goods or services in question. There should be no cross-subsidies from one group of consumers to another, and any activity that builds up a profit should respond by reducing its prices. No losses on any activity should be countenanced. A public enterprise may be able to 'break even' at several levels of activity. The maximisation of consumers' surplus would provide a rule for choosing between such levels. Indeed, since there may be a bias at the present time towards choosing the level that involves least risk of failure or least managerial effort, such a rule could indicate a more rational and socially beneficial solution.

These formulations seem likely to do much towards clarifying the economic purposes of nationalised enterprises. The difficulties about 'wider obligations' that are non-economic or only partly economic in character remain, however. In practice, too, though no attempt to achieve maximum social surplus may be made, some non-consumer interests are always likely to make themselves felt.

When their contribution is assessed, the nature of the existing British nationalised industries should be borne in mind. They are all basic industries or services, part of the 'infra-structure' of the economy. Their status as public utilities was noted by the 1961 White Paper. Efficient low-cost production on their part can make a great contribution to the success of other economic activities. It should be emphasised, perhaps, that the return-on-capital standard (implying a limited rate of profit) announced in the White Paper is a pragmatic device set up for administrative convenience. At the present time it suits the industries; but it will obviously be possible to raise or lower (or remove) the rate of profit in the future – the industries are not enjoined to secure *maximum* profits. The question in this chapter is, what principles should politicians and civil servants have in mind in fixing such standards?

Economic aims, however widely defined, cannot provide all the answers all the time. Insistence on them, narrowly defined, breeds criticism of and hostility to industrial enterprises. It was in the attempt to establish a more acceptable conception that ideas of 'public interest' and 'public service' were developed. They embody the desire to serve rural consumers, poor consumers, and otherwise inconvenient consumers; and to operate in a fair and undiscriminating way. It has become clear that they are too vague to serve as working criteria for economic decisions. They demonstrate, however, that deliberately non-economic, let alone non-commercial, policies might be rationally pursued.

The upshot of all this seems to be as follows. First, the simplest criterion of policy is the strictly commercial test. Secondly, it is desirable, and is probably possible by cost-benefit analysis and similar techniques, to replace this in some cases by an economic criterion that embodies full social costs (and here the principle of maximum value-added is relevant). Thirdly, however, though less weight has been given to national-economy considerations since 1961, it is doubtful if they can be ignored altogether. And if long-term factors and social values are to play any part at all in administration and policy-making, it is hard to see that any single formula can be established for all circumstances. There is now, in America and Britain, a movement against defining business objectives in simple terms. It would be paradoxical if, at this juncture, crude commercial rules were prescribed for public enterprise. The best available objective, therefore, seems to be a general regard for economic ends, including all social costs, modified repeatedly by a variety of other considerations.

This may not seem a very remarkable conclusion. It is, however, a mistake to assume simplicity where there is in truth complexity; and since the nationalised industries are large organisations, affecting significantly many aspects of life, it is not surprising that their policies need to respect a variety of human ideals. Nevertheless, there is no need to let complexity degenerate into confusion. The nationalised industries should know where their commercial advantage lies; the social costs of likely policies should be carefully estimated where possible; and decisions involving other factors should be consciously taken and openly declared.

Several of the questions discussed in this chapter involve judgments about the sorts of relationships in society we consider desirable. For instance, emphasis on success by commercial standards often reflects a high valuation of wealth, especially material wealth. Stress

M

on public accountability and the pursuit of 'social' objectives, on the other hand, usually goes with a belief that fair and harmonious relationships among people are a main value. The problem of ultimate objectives is never a technical one—of *how* best to achieve something; it concerns, rather, how far one objective (such as increased wealth) should be pursued in comparison with other things. This is not to suggest that such things as increased wealth and social justice are always competitive: on the contrary, they are often connected. Moreover, other social values, such as liberty, may be at stake. These are formidable issues which obviously cannot be fully discussed here.

In any case, the determination of aims for any organisation— public or private, industrial or social—does not take place in a vacuum. The thinking of people in control is influenced by their environment, by the pressures they have to contend with. In nationalised industries, therefore, the boards' responsibility to the Government and the nation is a most pervasive factor; and the issues discussed in this chapter should always be related to the machinery of control and accountability described in Chapter 6.

At the beginning of this chapter it was pointed out that questions about the aims to be pursued, in nationalisation as elsewhere, readily become questions of social and political philosophy. This does not mean that they cannot be rationally discussed. There is in Britain sufficient consensus of opinion to make clarification and comparison of value judgements a worthwhile operation. Yet the common acceptance of a general liberalism as a social attitude does not mean that there are no underlying differences. Liberalism, after all, can be interpreted in various ways. Discussion of the aims of nationalisation is part of that interpretation.

8   The Politics of
Public Ownership

The main concern of this book has been to examine British nationalisation as it exists. It should be remembered, however, that problems
of policy and administration have been dealt with against a background of political disputation. It remains, therefore, to give an
account of developments in these controversies.

The concern with these matters is not an eccentricity of the British
political scene, the outcome of accidental prejudice. Nor is it an odd
quirk of history. In the circumstances of the age, the values esteemed
by radical and reformist temperaments led naturally to a preference
for public ownership. A tendency to mistrust the rich and powerful
brings a liking for a system in which such people are in some way
accountable. A habit of seeing issues in moral terms is readily
associated with systems based on co-operation 'for the good of all'
rather than private rivalry. Moreover, given a democratic political
system in which each person has one vote, the working classes have
obvious advantages in political control over industrial decisions,
compared with market control, where they are handicapped by
relative poverty. It is not difficult, therefore, to explain general
attitudes to the issues of public ownership without accepting
Marxist assumptions about social developments. These attitudes are
not universal—they are particularly weak in North America—but
they are widespread in most parts of the world.

In Britain and in other West European countries the range of
controversy has been narrowed in recent years. Socialist and
anti-socialist parties alike accept the 'mixed economy', in the sense
that all assume that some industries will be publicly owned while
others remain in private hands. Yet considerable differences still
remain over the extent of public enterprise and the way in which

existing nationalisation is to be run. There have been many hopes
and predictions that the controversy would fade away entirely.
It has not yet done so; and the narrowing of the gap between
the views of the main British parties does not necessarily make
the issue less divisive. Only when issues are replaced by other
controversies, arousing stronger emotions, are they effectively
superseded.

At the beginning of the book, R. H. Tawney's distinction between
questions of ownership and those of administration was quoted
(see p. 15). In the previous three chapters, questions of administration in one form or another have been considered. These concluding
pages return to the question of ownership itself.

Labour Party attitudes

It is convenient to begin the discussion with the Labour Party,
although it has been in opposition for most of the time since the
industries were nationalised. As the Party favourably disposed
towards public ownership, it has spent most time discussing it, and
there are in fact considerable developments in attitude to record.

In Chapter 2 it was noted that the Party eventually adopted
the public corporation as its method of nationalisation, and gave
priority to the basic industries in its programme of action. In its
professions of socialist faith the Party had always stressed two
things: that it was democratic and would govern by parliamentary
means; and that it was gradualist and would socialise industry only
in stages.

This doctrine of 'gradualism' served as a policy of moderation in
the 1930s. It ensured that the programme of 1945 was practicable and
capable of execution by ordinary legislation. The 'stage by stage'
idea, however, implied that the first nationalisation programme
would be succeeded by others. It was necessary therefore for the
Party to prepare new policies on nationalisation for the election of
1950. There were in the preparation of these policies the first signs of
disagreements in the Party about nationalisation, which were to
persist for the next ten years. Briefly, the more cautious Labour
politicians stressed the need for consolidation and the effective

development of existing nationalisation—for instance, the integration of transport envisaged by the 1947 Act had scarcely begun. The left wing in the Party, however, was anxious that the momentum of 1945–50 should not be lost, and that further progress should be made, in the event of success at the polls in 1950.

The programme for the election of February 1950 was therefore something of a compromise, though it appears radical enough today. The election manifesto proposed that public ownership in one form or another should be extended to beet-sugar manufacture and sugar refining; to the cement industry; to 'appropriate sections' of the chemical industry; to meat wholesaling and cold storage; to water supply; and to 'all suitable minerals'. It also declared that 'monopoly concerns which cannot be dealt with in other ways will be socialised.'[1] One of its most interesting proposals, however, was that for industrial assurance, where it suggested mutual ownership by the policy-holders. Ownership of insurance companies transacting life-assurance business by the weekly collection method was to be transferred from shareholders to the policy-holders themselves, not to the Government or a public corporation.[2]

The General Election of 1950 was won by the Labour Party very narrowly, and no legislation in this field was practicable, though the already enacted nationalisation of steel was carried out. At the election of October 1951 the Party made no specific nationalisation proposals, and the Conservatives were narrowly victorious. The legislative situation was therefore reversed, and debate in the House of Commons centred on the denationalisation of steel and road haulage in 1953. The difficulties of the Labour Party at this time were accentuated by its divided counsels. The left wing of the party, inspired by Aneurin Bevan, was pressing for radical policies in foreign and defence affairs as well as in industry. The nature of these internal conflicts may be judged from two documents appearing in the same year. In 1953 the Trades Union Congress published a report on public ownership.[3] This was a cautious document which, though it commended existing nationalisation as a success, displayed no great enthusiasm for its extension. Explicitly it favoured nationalisation of water supply and the extension of the frontier of the

National Coal Board to include some manufacturers of mining machinery. The attitude of the T.U.C. in this document (accepted by the 1953 Congress in Douglas) was cooler than that of many constituent unions, and the Confederation of Shipbuilding and Engineering Unions in particular favoured further wide measures of public ownership, including aircraft construction, the machine-tool industry, shipping and shipbuilding. The Labour Party itself issued a policy document in June 1953 setting out another group of proposals.[4] Steel and many road-haulage units were to be renationalised, and the State was to have power to 'build and operate new enterprises, or acquire a controlling interest in existing enterprises, or both'. This referred in particular to sections of the engineering industry, to key machine-tool firms, and to a substantial degree of the chemical industry. The beet-sugar monopoly and water supply were also to be taken over, and a controlling interest acquired in a few firms making mining machinery. Industrial assurance would become a publicly organised service, and the State might manufacture requirements for the National Health Service.

In the General Election of 1955, which followed this programme, the Labour Party did badly and the Conservatives increased their majority. The proposals therefore came to nothing. A few months after the election, C. R. Attlee resigned as leader of the Labour Party, a position he had held since 1935, and Hugh Gaitskell was elected in his place.

A new approach?

A period of more fundamental discussion about public ownership now began. It was no longer a question of revising and adjusting a programme, but of examining the purpose of the whole line of policy. Unfortunately the Labour Party was only in moderate shape to do this. The leadership issue had been settled, but many of the disagreements and animosities were still little concealed. So far as public ownership was concerned, there was division between those who wished for considerable changes in attitude (eventually called the 'revisionists')[5] and those who believed in a reassertion of traditional principles, who became known as 'fundamentalists'.

It would be misleading to suggest that the disagreements were often clear-cut: indeed, it sometimes appeared that there were as many views as there were Labour politicians. The outlines of the revisionist case, however, became generally familiar. Socialism, it was argued, is not synonymous with public ownership. It consists of a set of values, of which social equality is probably the most distinctive. Public ownership, or nationalisation, is a means to these ends. But, the revisionists said, it is not the only means, nor is it certain that mere transference to public ownership will by itself promote the ideals very much.

One of the grounds for supposing that nationalisation promotes social equality is that it eliminates industries as sources of unearned income and capital gains for private individuals. In 1953 Mr John Strachey wrote:

Socialists are determined to redistribute the national income not only more equally, but above all more justly . . . The only final way of doing this is to do it 'at source' : to transfer to the people, that is to say, the ownership of the source of the major unearned incomes which at present flow to the shareholding and property holding classes.[6]

In practice, argued the revisionists, the results of this brave doctrine were not so clear. Nationalisation in Britain involves paying compensation to the former owners, who can reinvest it elsewhere and so maintain their advantages. Further capital for the industries is raised by borrowing, even if indirectly. There is some progress towards equality, indeed, because the interest paid by the industries is less than the distributed dividends would have been. But the effect is not large, and anyway progress towards social justice by this method is likely to be slow and cumbersome.

Another ethical argument for nationalisation was that it substituted co-operation for conflict and competition. To this the revisionists replied that the elimination of competition did not by itself ensure a co-operative spirit in industry. In fact some rivalry and emulation were, on balance, desirable, and competition as such was valuable in many circumstances.

Other traditional arguments for nationalisation were more practical and less idealistic in character. Some—such as the view that
basic industries or monopolies ought to be controlled by the community—applied only to particular industries. Others, such as the
need to improve efficiency, to co-operate in national planning, or to
improve labour relations, might conceivably be achieved in other
ways. All in all, it was argued, developments in mid-century had
'weakened but not destroyed' the case for general nationalisation.[7]
The situation, in the revisionist view, gave rise to a need to modify
and re-present the habitual Labour Party approach to nationalisation.
The new outlook had two main aspects, one of which at least
carried assent well beyond that of the more determined revisionists.

First, then, it was necessary to vary the methods of public ownership. 'Nationalisation', in the sense of national ownership of whole
industries, should apply only in one or two more cases than at
present. Municipal ownership, co-operative ownership, and
ownership of competitive enterprises were to be stressed, and new
forms were to be sought. In particular, the preparation of lists of
industries scheduled for nationalisation—known as 'shopping lists'—
was to be stopped.

The second ambition of the revisionists brought sharper resistance
in the Party from the fundamentalists. This was to reduce the
promotion of public ownership from its central place in Labour
policies to the status of 'one policy among others'. Stress was to be
put on other measures—fiscal reform, educational changes, development of the social services—and public ownership advocated only
in relation to other particular ends, not for its own sake. The mixed
economy was to be recognised as permanent.

In the period after 1955 an attempt was made by the Labour Party
to take stock of these views, and to resolve conflict in the Party by
a process of full discussion, directed especially to framing new,
agreed, policies. Out of this process there emerged two policy
statements about public ownership.

The first of these was a review of the existing nationalised industries called *Public Enterprise*. The Party had formed no dramatic
new attitudes; no structural changes were proposed, but it was hoped

that the machinery for consumer representation would be more effective.

The other statement, *Industry and Society*, was more adventurous and more controversial. It analysed the changes that had been taking place in industrial capitalism, and emphasised the distinctive nature of the large firm. A few hundred large companies dominated the economy, and were responsible for about half the investment and profits of the private sector. In these firms ownership had become separated from control, and, moreover, they obtained much of their investment funds from internal sources. National full-employment policies, ensuring high demand, meant that the prosperity of these firms was to a great extent underwritten by the Government.

The actual proposals of this statement stressed, as expected, the need for a variety of forms of public ownership. The Companies' Acts should be reviewed to develop more definite forms of public accountability, and a code of conduct should be set out to promote desirable social practices in industry. Besides the renationalisation of steel and long-distance road haulage, public ownership might be extended in 'any industry or part of industry which, after thorough inquiry, is found to be seriously failing the nation'. Thus reports like those of the McGowan, Heyworth, and Reid committees (discussed in Chapter 3) might again lead to nationalisation. But the acquisition of firms, rather than industries, was a possible solution. The State should also participate in expansion and development by providing equity capital—that is, by making investments that receive a share of profits (instead of only providing fixed-interest loans) for new or existing enterprises. Furthermore, the pamphlet proposed the deliberate acquisition of shares in existing private-enterprise concerns, by accepting them in lieu of cash for death duties, or by investing social-security funds in industry.

These last proposals were the source of much dispute. The reason for including them was that they would promote equality, in spite of the doubts that had been expressed about the effectiveness of public ownership in this matter. In fact, it was the need to ensure a share in capital gains (rather than current profits) for the community at large that was stressed. Through share ownership a proportion of the increasing *wealth* of industry would become available for community purposes.

Though the statement had been agreed by a committee from all wings of the Party, it did not please most of the left when published. In its acceptance of the mixed economy and the absence of precise proposals for large-scale take-overs they detected a weakening of socialist purpose. Share-buying did not give active control either to the Government or the workers, and it might commit the Government too closely to the outlook and interests of private business, rather than help to modify the behaviour of such concerns. At the Labour Party Conference in 1957 at Brighton there was an attempt to reject the statement as lacking the 'rich red blood of Socialist objective';[8] it was carried, however, and formed the basis of the Labour Party programme at the General Election of 1959.

Unlike the left wing of the Labour Party, the Conservative Party and private industry professed to see no moderation in the new policy. The discussion of the large firm and the share-buying programme were linked in allegations that all large firms were to be nationalised; and the criterion of 'failing the nation' was attacked for its vagueness. In the event, the Conservatives were victorious again in 1959, with an increased majority.

This third defeat brought on an unhappy period of recrimination and dispute in the Labour Party. It was felt by many leaders that what was wrong was not so much policies as the traditional party 'image'. As a contribution to the presentation of a transformed view of the Party to the public, its leader, Hugh Gaitskell, proposed the repeal of Clause Four of the Party Constitution (see Chapter 2, p. 21), which stated the objects of the Party almost entirely in terms of common ownership. (By this time, 'distribution and exchange' had been added to 'the means of production'.) In fact, sufficient support for a change was not forthcoming, and the attempt was dropped in the summer of 1960. In this connection, however, a longer statement of Party objectives was formulated and approved by the Party Conference at Scarborough in 1960. This succeeded in placing public ownership as one aim among others. Two items in the declaration stated that the Labour Party

(i) ... stands for democracy in industry, and for the right of the workers both in the public and private sectors to full consultation in all the vital decisions of management, especially those affecting conditions of work.

(j) It is convinced that these social and economic objectives can be achieved only through an expansion of common ownership substantial enough to give the community power over the commanding heights of the economy. Common ownership takes varying forms, including state-owned industries and firms, producer and consumer co-operation, municipal ownership and public participation in private concerns. Recognising that both public and private enterprise have a place in the economy it believes that further extension of common ownership should be decided from time to time in the light of these objectives and according to circumstances, with due regard for the views of the workers and consumers concerned.

The relationship of this declaration to Clause Four (still retained) is obscure. But the declaration was stated to refer to 'the second half of the twentieth century', so perhaps Clause Four is consigned to the remoter future. Election propaganda apart, it is clear that what are really important are the immediate programmes of the Party, and indeed whether it may be practicable in office for these to be carried out.

In 1961 the Labour Party published *Signposts for the Sixties*, and its programme for the 1964 election followed lines foreshadowed there, stressing the need to increase the rate of economic growth by mobilising technological resources. The manifesto for the election stated:

The public sector will make a vital contribution to the national plan. We will have a co-ordinated policy for the major fuel industries. Major expansion programmes will be needed in the existing nationalised industries, and they will be encouraged, with the removal of the present restrictions placed upon them, to diversify and move into new fields: for example, the railways' workshops will be free to seek export markets, and the National Coal Board to manufacture the machinery and equipment it needs. Private monopoly in steel will be replaced by public ownership and control. The water supply industry, most of which is already owned by the community, will be reorganised under full public ownership.

The manifesto also stated that, to ensure that new scientific discoveries were rapidly applied to industry, the Government would establish new industries 'either by public enterprise or in partnership with private industry'. The Labour Party also promised a national plan for transport, with regional planning authorities drawing up plans for their areas, major rail closures being halted meanwhile. British Road Services would be given power to extend their fleet of vehicles. The proposals in the manifesto for a Land Commission also involved an element of public ownership, in that land being redeveloped would come into the ownership of the Commission.[9]

The Labour Party under the leadership of Harold Wilson[10] won the General Election of October 1964, but had a majority of only four over the other parties in the House of Commons. In these circumstances the development of legislative action in relation to public ownership was under some constraint. There were, however, in 1965 and 1966 many indications of new attitudes at work. The White Paper on *Steel Nationalisation* of April 1965 proposed the setting up of a large public corporation, but it was not to be a monopolistic one, and it was to be encouraged to pursue ancillary activities. Similarly the existing nationalised concerns were given permission to widen and diversify their activities. The concept of the corporations as vehicles for 'the administration of industries' seemed to have given way to one which regarded them as large 'public firms'. In December 1965 the Government joined with private investors and two trade unions in providing equity and loan capital sufficient to save the Fairfield Shipbuilding and Engineering Company, of Glasgow, from bankruptcy, and to provide for its continued operation under new management and with new understandings about labour relations. In 1966 there were proposals for a Government agency which, acting as a holding company, would provide capital for existing firms, found new ones, and foster desirable mergers.

At all events, the arrival of a Labour Government is likely to consolidate the fourth period in the history of British public ownership, which began in about 1955. In Chapter 2 the first three were described. They were marked out by the Government department, schemes of joint control, and the public corporation as the favoured technique of nationalisation. The less emphatic but more varied approach now favoured must serve as a guide to a new period of Government action.

If the Labour Party does succeed in substantially carrying out its present programme, then, as a reforming party, it will need another programme. This will mean deciding whether to proceed a further stage on the present road, or whether to seek new directions. Decisions of this type are never easy for any party.

Conservative Party attitudes

The Conservative Party has not grown any more sympathetic towards public ownership in the last twenty years.

In Chapter 2 it was noted that several of the pre-war public corporations were set up under Conservative auspices, and this at least implied that they might regard public ownership as appropriate in special circumstances. The Conservatives did not propose any nationalisation at the 1945 election, but their opposition to some items in the Labour programme — the Bank of England, the coal mines, electricity — was not particularly vigorous. Transport, especially road haulage, and steel were different matters. The Conservative Party in Parliament used all the means available to resist and delay these measures, supported by the propaganda of the industries outside Parliament.

During these years the Conservatives had to formulate a long-term attitude to public ownership in the changed circumstances. There was a general movement of public opinion during the war which had to be taken into account, and the Labour Party in office had succeeded in establishing a number of new public corporations. It is the chief glory of British conservatism, as distinct from other right-wing doctrines, that it adapts itself to changing situations. The period of opposition from 1945 to 1951 was a time when adaptation was crucial for the future of the Party.

In the event, the Conservative rethinking –led and encouraged by Mr R. A. Butler –achieved a remarkably coherent (and electorally successful) set of principles. The social-service reforms of the Labour Government were on the whole accepted and even welcomed. Most of their nationalisation measures were also accepted –but grudgingly, on the argument that 'eggs cannot be unscrambled'. Steel and road haulage were to be returned to private enterprise and the administration of the rest improved. Moreover, the Conservative Party accepted the doctrine of competition in industry more openly than it had ever done before. One consequence of this outlook has been that, though Conservative publicity now stresses the share of the Party in building the welfare state, in developing economic planning, and even in trade union legislation, little attention is given to the creation of the public corporation.[11]

In July 1949 the Conservative Party published a pamphlet *The Right Road for Britain*, setting out policies for the forthcoming election. It declared firmly:

> The Conservative Party will undertake no further nationalisa-
> tion. It will restore free enterprise where that is practicable. But
> we refuse at this time of economic danger to aggravate industrial
> discord. We must ensure that those in control of vital industries
> are not persistently distracted from their task of management by
> watching the political weather. We have therefore no other
> course but to leave some industries nationalised but we shall
> radically overhaul their organisation to make them more
> human, less centralised and more efficient.[12]

The iron and steel industry, road transport, and the purchase of raw cotton were specifically marked for denationalisation. The re-organisation of the existing corporations would embody 'the greatest degree of decentralisation', and parliamentary control would be strengthened.

This formula served the Conservative Party until 1964: maintenance of the existing nationalised industries, but fierce hostility to any further extension. Many of the detailed proposals in the pamphlet, such as abolishing the divisional boards in the coal industry, and making more use of independent price tribunals, came to nothing; and as described in Chapter 3, denationalisation did not proceed quite so far as at first envisaged in either steel or road haulage; but broadly speaking, the doctrine of 1949 had not, by 1964, needed much further adaptation. It remained the essence of the Conservative position at the elections of 1955, 1959, and 1964. The 1964 manifesto stated that:

> The Conservative Party is utterly opposed to any extension of nationalisation, whether outright or piecemeal. We propose to complete the denationalisation of steel. Industries in public ownership will continue to be developed as modern businesses.[13]

Since the Conservative Party was in office from 1951 until 1964, its attitudes have been reflected in the actions of the Government, and the most significant of these have emerged in previous chapters. The outlook of the Party, as it manifested itself on the back benches and in the country, however, may be indicated. There was of course pressure on the Government to achieve the promised degree of denationalisation, and there have been rumblings of discontent that it has not gone further — in particular, about the remnant of the steel industry still publicly owned in 1964.

The first Party belief about the existing industries was that they were vastly overcentralised. The Conservatives saw themselves as the defenders of freedom, and hence of the diffusion of power in the community. This principle meant decentralisation and local responsibility within the new organisations. The break-up of the Transport Commission, the various changes in railway administration, and perhaps the reorganisation of electricity in 1957 can be seen as consequences of this belief. As a political dogma, however, it met its Waterloo with the publication of the Fleck report on the organisation of the Coal Board in 1955, in which leading industrialists declared that decentralisation in the industry was already excessive. Conservatives still tend to prefer decentralised arrangements, but they no longer expect large changes to be easily possible.

A second Conservative idea was that the industries should as far as possible be subjected to competition, either between themselves or from private enterprise. This idea sprang from the enhanced prominence in Conservative thinking given to competition since the war. It was not possible to advocate uninhibited private enterprise without also emphasising the virtues of competition, and to most members of the Conservative Party it seemed desirable to extend the competition as far as possible into the nationalised industries. The Government was able to carry this out in many cases, as described in Chapter 7, though there is some effective monopoly and protection left. The independent airlines, the fuel-oil industry, and private road transport all made strong challenges in markets that were formerly the preserve of nationalised industries. The establishment of the Independent Television Authority in 1956 was a further example of the adoption of competitive and commercial arrangements.

The strictly commercial approach, propounded in the Herbert report and elsewhere, also had strong attractions for the Conservative Party, and it has often been warmly advocated from the back benches. Nevertheless, the Government has never been able to adopt it in full, owing to the difficulties described in Chapter 7. Many back-bench Members of Parliament, too, have felt the need for exceptions on matters such as branch-line closures, where serious social effects became plain.

The Conservative Party in Parliament can claim to have played a constructive and successful part in the development of public accountability, notably with the Select Committee on Nationalised Industries and the increased information on public investment.

Labour M.P.s felt that such investigations were intended as muck-raking expeditions, and were often overcautious in their attitude; Conservatives had no such reservations.

The future Conservative attitude is difficult to discern. So long as the standstill held, and was electorally attractive, there was little point in changing. If the Party proceeds to adopt more radically free-enterprise policies, as some within it suggest, then it is difficult to see that very much more can be done to public enterprise without structural change — though some further opportunities of extending competition from outside may arise. If there is more nationalisation, by a Labour Government, then the question of eventual acceptance by the Conservatives arises; there is no doubt that they will vigorously oppose it in the early stages. Will they denationalise steel a second time?[14] And what will they do about variants, such as governmental share-buying or competitive, publicly owned businesses, if these are put into practice?

At General Elections since 1950 the Conservative Party has made much of the alleged inefficiency of nationalisation. This in theory should put those Ministers responsible for public enterprises in difficulties, since charges of inefficiency should be laid at their door. In practice, the Conservatives have managed this ambivalence very well, perhaps because their critics have often found themselves in the converse difficulty — of trying to attack ministerial policies without damaging the principle of nationalisation itself.

Conservative Party attitudes have been generally aligned, of course, with those of private industry, particularly at election times. These are discussed below.

Liberal Party attitudes

The Liberal Party grew and prospered in the nineteenth century as the party of the industrial middle class, and its economic attitudes traditionally favoured freedom of enterprise and competition. It developed considerably, however, from being a laissez-faire party, and between the wars it played a part in fashioning the idea of the public corporation. It was also the party of Keynes and Beveridge, the formulators of the economic strategy for full employment.

In the 1940s it adopted a pragmatic attitude to nationalisation, as distinct from what it regarded as Labour Party dogmatism. In Parliament it supported some Bills and opposed others, as described in Chapter 3. Steel nationalisation was strongly opposed, and though in principle the Party retains a non-dogmatic attitude, it has not found it necessary to advocate any measures of public ownership since 1950. It is even more strongly attached than the Conservative Party to ideas of competition and free trade in industry, and stresses the need to remove any form of protection to public enterprise. In the late 1950s and 1960s it convinced itself that this coolness towards public ownership would enable it to become a great radical party of the left.

The Liberal Party's programme for the 1964 election made only a brief reference to public ownership. It declared that:

> The wrangle about nationalisation and denationalisation is irrelevant to most of the problems of modern industry.
>
> Liberals want a truce in the dispute over steel which will take the industry out of politics and enable it to get on with the job. We press instead for modernisation of the industry, Government help for redundancy, competitive marketing, and a World Steel Conference to cut tariffs and agree on world rules of competition.[15]

In August 1964 a Liberal working party produced a report which tried to find a 'third way' for steel. It suggested that a possible compromise might be found in State shareholdings in four 'pace-setting' firms. These part-public enterprises would be in competition with the rest of the industry, which would still be privately owned.[16] Though this had not become official Liberal policy by the time of the election, it did reveal a readiness to accept the relevance of public ownership, albeit in a very limited form, in special circumstances. Both before and after the election, however, the Liberal Party made it clear that it would oppose Labour Party proposals for the full renationalisation of the steel industry, and it was hostile to the eventual proposals of April 1965.

Industrial opposition

An account of political attitudes to public ownership must include the opposition of private enterprise. Though not formally affiliated to the Conservative Party, industrial organisations usually find themselves in harmony with its major economic policies. Certainly they emphatically endorse its hostility to extensions of public ownership.

The steel industry has been most involved. The nationalisation of steel was proposed by many socialist writers before 1939, and its inclusion in the Labour Party's 1945 programme set in train the events leading to the nationalisation and denationalisation described in Chapter 3. Ever since then, the return of the industry to public ownership has been at the head of all the Party's programmes, revisionist as they may be. As a result, relations between the industry's leaders and the Labour Party have become embittered. In principle the industry was not opposed to public control, but the breakdown of attempts at compromise in 1948 produced an atmosphere of hostility which has never departed. The Labour Party was confirmed in its attitude by the refusal of steel businessmen to co-operate with the nationalised Iron and Steel Corporation in 1950–52; by the Conservatives' Act of denationalisation without giving the Corporation a chance to become effective; and by the flow of the industry's propaganda since. Before the General Elections of 1959 and 1964, the industry conducted very extensive advertising campaigns both through its trade association, the British Iron and Steel Federation, and individual firms. These were supplemented by surveys and other public-relations techniques, designed to show not only the folly but also the unpopularity of nationalisation. The steel industry is also believed to make substantial financial contributions to the general anti-nationalisation propaganda mentioned below.

The wisdom of this policy depends on its electoral effectiveness: if sufficient voters were affected by it to keep the Labour Party out of office, it might well be considered worth while. The Labour Party, however, regards the campaigns as intimidation and 'political blackmail', and the emotions they arouse in Party loyalists are hardly such as to allow the leaders to change their intentions even if they wanted. Whether the narrow result of October 1964 justified the industry's expenditure or not is a matter of conjecture.

Other industries and other organisations have also carried out anti-nationalisation propaganda. The vigorous efforts in the late 1940s of the Road Haulage Association were mentioned in Chapter 3. Before the 1950 election, campaigns were organised with considerable skill by the sugar, cement, and insurance companies, and these have been followed by extensive Press advertising, by industry, critical of nationalisation, in every pre-election period. This now tends to be of a general character, and is promoted by an organisation called 'Aims of Industry'.[17] Many private businesses are also believed to contribute to the funds of the Conservative Party, either directly or through a body called British United Industrialists.

The Labour Party's response to this flow of hostile propaganda has been to complain about the use of company funds (rather than personal wealth) for political purposes, and in particular about the secrecy with which this is done. Companies do not normally disclose subscriptions to political groups, nor does the Conservative Party publish its accounts. Finance apart, however, political advertising is scarcely a very secret activity. Nor is there any doubt about its legality, since it can obviously be claimed to be in the interests of the companies. Officially, the advertising campaigns are against nationalisation and not against the Labour Party as such; the industrial subscriptions to the Conservative Party are presumably intended to have a more general impact.

The Federation of British Industries, the main top-level trade association of British industry, does not normally take part in partisan controversy. In 1958, however, it published a pamphlet setting out its views.[18] It did not recommend the denationalisation of any industries already nationalised, 'but the country ought not to be content with their performance so far'. They had not met their financial obligations; they had maintained low prices irrespective of costs; and they had taken a more than proportionate share of national investment funds. The position of free enterprise, which worked in a 'dominant climate' of competition, was contrasted; there, the yardstick of profitability provided a clear measure of efficiency. The merit of the pamphlet lay in its point-by-point exposition of the whole range of anti-nationalisation arguments; but a crucial weakness was its failure to acknowledge sufficiently the influence of Government policies on the results achieved by the industries.

There is, of course, no counter-attack from the nationalised industries. Their constitutional position prevents them from indulging in very active political propaganda, though there is some prestige advertising. In defending themselves from nationalisation, private-enterprise firms constantly criticise existing public enterprise, and so damage the general standing of the industries. It would scarcely be possible—even with a sympathetic Government—for public corporations to indulge in anti-capitalist advertising campaigns, but it might be possible to allow them to play a more direct part in protecting their own public reputations.

A further sphere of influence has opened to the nationalised industries in recent years. In 1965 the Federation of British Industries merged with some other employers' organisations to form the Confederation of British Industry. In January 1966 it was announced that the main nationalised industries were joining the C.B.I. as 'industrial associates' (though London Transport remained outside). They would take a full part in committee work and pay full subscriptions, but would not have voting rights on the Confederation's council. In principle, therefore, the C.B.I. remained the spokesman of private enterprise, and it remains to be seen how much effect the entry of the nationalised bodies has on its general attitudes.

Harold Laski's thesis

In the 1930s the left wing of the Labour Party was inclined to doubt the practicability of socialist reforms, including large-scale public ownership, by conventional parliamentary means. These views were most forcibly expressed by Harold Laski in successive books and pamphlets.[19] The argument followed Marxist lines: if a group of people found its vital interests at stake, then it would take desperate measures, perhaps including violence, to protect them. The owners of industry naturally regarded public ownership as a threat to their fundamental position, and therefore they were unlikely to acquiesce merely because constitutionally elected socialists had legislated to this effect. Accordingly, a Labour Government should be prepared for non-co-operation, sabotage, and possibly violent resistance. It should not be deterred from its course; it should be prepared to govern by emergency decree, and to meet force with force.

The experience of 1945-51 is generally regarded as disproving this thesis. Certainly it shows that under certain political conditions much nationalisation can be carried out by orthodox legislation. It does not show, however, that any amount of public ownership can be achieved merely on the basis of a Government's constitutional prerogatives.

The non-co-operation of the steel industry in 1951 and the pre-election publicity campaigns might be held to give some support to a modified version of the theory. Certainly the controllers of private enterprise regard nationalisation as a measure of an altogether different character from other industrial policies. It does not remove all of them from their posts, for high management posts must be held by people of the best quality available. Moreover, shareholders are fully compensated. But nationalisation alters the basis of the controllers' authority, the conditions of their tenure, and the extent of their accountability; in short, it strikes at their fundamental power. In these circumstances, a nationalising party must expect determined opposition, which is not confined to other political parties.

The behaviour of any industries that may be faced in the future with nationalisation is a matter for speculation. Though formidable in electoral terms, their opposition so far has been legal and constitutional, and seems likely to continue so. The situation can perhaps be assessed thus. The response of industrialists to the prospect of nationalisation will be vigorous, but will remain peaceful and constitutional, provided that the transfers to public ownership are limited in scale, carry compensation, and have a Government with moral as well as formal authority behind them. More extreme programmes might bring more extreme reactions. If Laski meant that *any* nationalisation would be regarded as provocation to violence, then this is clearly untrue: but there is little doubt that industrialists take to political action (at least in so far as it includes hostile propaganda and non-co-operation) more readily in the face of nationalisation than they do when faced with, say, heavy taxation. It is the strength of this sort of opposition that constitutes the real problem for the Labour Party in the 1960s. The question of full-blooded opposition to a red-blooded programme has now become remote from practical politics. The question of whether even a relatively moderate programme can be achieved against the pervasive influence of private industry is still before us.

Further possibilities

The origins of nationalisation as a protest against capitalist control of industrial enterprises were discussed in Chapter 3. As indicated, there are other possible ways of reforming industrial ownership, and in recent years there has been a revival of interest in other methods of changing the structure of the firm. These proposals have in common an insistence on treating the existing firm as the appropriate unit of control. They eschew any drastic revision of industrial structure such as accompanied nationalisation by the public-corporation method. They are compatible with the retention of a competitive system in the economy, though the incentives and style of competition might be modified by some of the more radical schemes.

It is convenient to classify the various suggestions by relating them to the conventional political spectrum, but this should not be interpreted rigidly: there is considerable overlap and variation; moreover, in all parties there is some mistrust of this approach in any form.

First, there is 'wider shareholding'. A variety of schemes have been put forward which make easier the acquisition of shares in public companies. It is hoped by this means to end the feeling that capitalist ownership puts industry into the hands of a small, wealthy group; instead, ownership will be diffused through the community, and its benefits (and outlook) will be widely shared. Unit trusts, which hold shares in a large number of individual companies, enable a person investing a small amount not only to spread the risks, but also to have this investment managed by experts. There are also methods of buying shares by small regular subscriptions.

A variant of this idea is 'employee-shareholding'. In these cases a company makes it possible for its employees to obtain its shares on specially favourable terms; they may be issued as a form of payment to established employees. A worker is thus enabled to acquire a 'stake' in his company and to share in its profits. If his shares carry voting rights, he also becomes a member of its ultimate controlling body.

These are the types of proposals most favoured by Conservative currents of opinion. It should be noted that such schemes do not disturb the principle of capitalist control at all. The benefits and rights of shareholders are made available to more people, but it is only by virtue of capital holdings that their position is improved. However, the more shareholders there are for any particular enterprise, the more difficult it is for shareholder control to be effective, and the stronger the position of the directors and managers. It has also been argued that the financial gains of employee-shareholders are no more than a variant of higher wage and salary payments.[20]

However, if employee-shareholding is carried out in an extensive and radical fashion, it can give workers a substantial part in the control of a company, and there are a few firms in which share-holding or partnership does make a real difference to the structure of the enterprise. A more fundamental charge, giving rights to employees as such, would require legislation. In Western Germany a system of co-determination giving such rights has been established. In Britain the Liberal Party has declared its belief in *co-ownership*. This implied at first support for schemes of profit-sharing, employee-shareholding, and co-partnership as they already existed. But in 1962 a report on *Industrial Affairs* carried the Party much further.[21] It proposed that the directors of public companies should be chosen by annual representative meetings, composed half of the representatives of shareholders and half of representatives of established employees. Thus workers would have a strong, if indirect, voice in the control of the firm. In addition, the Board of Trade would have the right to nominate spokesmen for the public interest at company meetings.

The Labour Party remains mainly concerned with public ownership as such. The ideas of consumer co-operation and of full workers' control are, of course, associated with the Labour movement, and there have recently been some notable attempts to explore again the possibilities of this type of reform. A Fabian Society pamphlet, *The Company and the Community* by Paul Derrick, has proposed 'the socialisation of the company'. This involves limiting 'the return to the shareholder so that he ceases to be an owner and becomes a creditor'. Tax differentials would be arranged so that companies were encouraged to convert themselves into fixed-return corporations. New representative bodies within the firm would help to limit the power of management. Another Fabian pamphlet, *The Democratic Firm* by Norman Ross, presented an analysis of the enterprise as 'a complex of group relationships in which conflicting objectives can and usually do exist'. The need was to create a system for the effective adjustment of these differing interests. The pamphlet proposed a supervisory representative council composed of shareholders' representatives and employee representatives in proportions which reflected their contribution to the income generated by the enterprise, as measured by net profits on the one hand and wages and salaries on the other. Though these Fabian schemes have some similarity to earlier proposals and to practice abroad, they embody the political values of the left by effecting a sharp reduction (on balance) in the power of the shareholders compared with that of employees or other groups.[22]

It must be noted that all these proposals would leave the structure of industry much as it is. They do not involve any change in Government control, nor do they contribute to improved economic planning. Few of them embody arrangements for public accountability. In so far as nationalisation does deal with this sort of problem, therefore, the reform of the enterprise is not in the same field and does not undertake the same tasks. It is relevant, however, to the problem of industrial ownership conceived as a problem of social relationships and political power. Thus there are currents of opinion in all parties that acknowledge the need for changes in industry not primarily designed to improve its efficiency.

In fact, the main political activity of the 1960s in Britain is concerned with economic growth and economic planning. The establishment of the National Economic Development Council, the attempt to secure an incomes policy, the work of the Department of Economic Affairs, and the preoccupation with technological advance are all matters related to the economy as a whole. In the current political context, therefore, public enterprise is judged by its contribution to these economic ends.

The urgency of these problems is not to be denied. Nevertheless, it would be wrong to forget that public ownership sprang as much from criticisms of the injustice of capitalism as from its alleged inefficiency. In the long run, the social and political aspects of the control of industry may not continue to be overshadowed by the economic.

Public ownership remains, in Britain, a party matter. There is great virtue in this. It brings the issues into the open. It means that few aspects are left obscure or unexamined by one controversialist or another. It is highly desirable that great industrial problems should receive the publicity and scrutiny that political debate ensures. Yet there is a danger of over-simplification. Many people will decide to oppose public ownership on principle. In doing so, they should be aware of the problems with which it attempts to deal; they should recognise that the question of how productive enterprises in society are to be controlled is one worthy of some attention, and that easy and dogmatic answers to it will certainly be unsatisfactory. In turn, those who support further public ownership should remember that, as a change from the existing situation, it needs to have a case made for it. It is presented as a remedy for alleged evils: economic, social and political. Its advocates have a duty to see that the forms it takes and the ways in which it operates ensure that it does in fact improve what it is meant to improve.

In short, nationalisation has been treated too much as an *either/or* question. There are many ways of owning and directing industrial enterprises, and an economic system could do worse than adopt a great variety of them.

Further Reading

There is a large literature on most aspects of nationalisation. Many of the more specific books and articles have been indicated in the end-notes to the text. Two major works, however, deserve special mention. The first is *Nationalised Industry and Public Owner-ship* by Professor W. A. Robson (Allen & Unwin, 2nd ed., 1962), a work of great scholarship and keen insight into many problems. It includes a complete bibliography of the subject up to the time of publication. The second main resource of the student is *Nationalisation — a book of readings*, edited by Professor A. H. Hanson (Allen & Unwin, 1963). This contains an invaluable collection of articles and excerpts, many of which would be otherwise almost inaccessible.

In addition there is a third textbook, *Government and Industry in Britain* by J. W. Grove (Longmans, 1962), which describes the full range of the British Government's concern with industrial affairs, and serves to put nationalisation in perspective with other forms of intervention.

On the early development of ideas about nationalisation and public ownership, the student should first consult H. E. Weiner, *British Labour and Public Ownership* (Stevens, 1960); G. N. Ostergaard's article, 'Labour and the development of the public corporation', in the *Manchester School* (May 1954); and W. A. Robson (ed.), *Public Enterprise* (Allen & Unwin, 1937).

Problems of organisation and administration are examined in the Fleck committee's report on 'The Organisation of the National Coal Board' (N.C.B., 1955) and the Herbert committee's report on 'The Electricity Supply Industry' (Cmd. 9672, 1956). Unofficial, radical criticism of the existing arrangements is found in H. A. Clegg and T. E. Chester, *The Future of Nationalisation* (Blackwell, 1953), and Lord Simon of Wythenshawe's pamphlet, *The Boards of Nationalised Industries* (Longmans, 1957).

The major discussion of public accountability is now found in A. H. Hanson, *Parliament and Public Ownership* (Cassell, 1961). Sir Toby Low's article on 'The Select Committee on Nationalised Industries' in *Public Administration* (Spring 1962) should also be consulted. The representation of consumers is examined by P. Sargant Florence and H. Maddick in an article on 'Consumers' Councils in the Nationalised Industries', in the *Political Quarterly* (July 1953), and in articles by G. Mills and M. Howe in *Public Administration* (Autumn 1960 and Spring 1964).

The official papers still relevant in 1966 include *Reorganisation of the Nationalised Transport Undertakings* (Cmnd. 1248, December 1960), the *Financial and Economic Obligations of the Nationalised Industries* (Cmnd. 1337, April 1961), *Steel Nationalisation* (Cmnd. 2651, April 1965), *Fuel Policy* (Cmnd. 2798, October 1965), and *The Finances of the Coal Industry* (Cmnd. 2805, November 1965). Detailed information on develop-ments in particular industries can be found in the Annual Reports and Accounts provided by all public corporations; in the reports of the Select Committee on Nationalised Industries; and in the annual reports of the various consumer and con-sultative councils. All these are House of Commons papers, obtainable from Govern-ment bookshops.

Critical accounts of nationalisation appear in R. Kelf-Cohen, *Nationalisation in Britain: the end of a dogma* (Macmillan, 2nd ed., 1961), and the Federation of British Industries' pamphlet, *Report on Nationalisation* (F.B.I., 1958).

Sympathetic reviews and criticisms can be found in the relevant chapters of C. A. R. Crosland's *The Future of Socialism* (Jonathan Cape, 1956); in John Hughes's pamphlet, *Nationalised Industries in the Mixed Economy* (Fabian Society, 1960), and in Michael Shanks (ed.), *Lessons of Public Enterprise* (Jonathan Cape, 1963).

Those interested mainly in economic problems of nationalised industries should read William G. Shepherd, *Economic Performance under Public Ownership — British Fuel and Power* (Yale, 1965); C. D. Foster, *The Transport Problem* (Blackie, 1963); K. M. Gwilliam, *Transport and Public Policy* (Allen & Unwin, 1964), and Stephen Wheatcroft, *Air Transport Policy* (Michael Joseph, 1964).

Notes

CHAPTER 2 : ORIGINS OF NATIONALISATION

1. R. H. Tawney, *The Acquisitive Society* (Bell, 1921), p. 149.

2. See M. Beer, *History of British Socialism* (Allen & Unwin, 1919); G. D. H. Cole, *History of Socialist Thought* (Macmillan, 1953–60); and Henry Pelling, *The Challenge of Socialism* (Black, 1954).

3. See, for example, F. A. Hayek (ed.), *Collectivist Economic Planning* (Routledge, 1935).

4. *Manchester Guardian*. December 5th, 1918.

5. It is not entirely clear what 'responsibility' entails in this context: certainly it is not now the automatic practice for Ministers to resign after administrative errors.

6. See G. B. Shaw, *The Commonsense of Municipal Trading* (Allen & Unwin, 1904).

7. See F. M. G. Willson, 'Ministries and Boards', *Public Administration* (Spring 1955).

8. Report of the Machinery of Government Committee (Cmd. 9230, 1918), p. 11.

9. Cmd. 2599.

10. This was a network of high-voltage transmission lines linking major power stations and so providing a unified source of supply for the whole country.

11. J. M. Keynes, 'The End of *Laissez-faire*', reprinted in *Essays in Persuasion* (Macmillan, 1931).

12. 'The public corporation has no shares and no shareholders, either public or private.' W. Friedmann, 'The New Public Corporations and the Law', *Modern Law Review* (1947), p. 235.

13. See D. N. Chester, 'The Public Corporations and the Classification of Administrative Bodies', *Political Studies* (February 1953).

CHAPTER 3 : MAJOR NATIONAL INDUSTRIES

1. Cmnd. 827.

2. *Conflict without Malice* (Odhams Press, 1955), p. 173.

3. Report of the Technical Advisory Committee on Coal Mining (Cmd. 6610, 1945).

4. *Hansard*, May 6th, 1946, col. 598.

5. Report of the committee of inquiry into the aircraft industry (Cmnd. 2853, December 1965).

6. At first there was a single Road Transport Executive, but in 1949 haulage and passenger interests were separated.

7. *Hansard*, December 17th, 1946, col. 1890.

8. This Act embodied proposals set out in a White Paper on *Reorganisation of the Nationalised Transport Undertakings* (Cmnd. 1248, 1960).

9. Cmd. 9672.

10. Cmd. 6699.

11. A general account of controversies up to 1951 is given in G. W. Ross, *The Nationalisation of Steel* (MacGibbon & Kee, 1965).

12. See Hugh Dalton, *High Tide and After* (Muller, 1962), Ch. xxx.

13. Cmnd. 2651.

14. The reader cannot do better than examine J. W. Grove's *Government and Industry in Britain* (Longmans, 1962).

15. The Atomic Energy Authority is chiefly concerned with prototypes; other nuclear power stations are built by consortia of private-enterprise firms.

16. Foreshadowed in a White Paper, *The Status of the Post Office* (Cmnd. 989, 1960).

CHAPTER 4 : PRACTICE OF NATIONALISATION

1. See White Paper on *The Finances of the Coal Industry* (Cmnd. 2805, November 1965).

2. The holders of L.P.T.B. stock had rights of action in the event of default, and for some types of stock there was the possibility of a bonus on the interest.

3. Cmnd. 1203.

4. Report of the Select Committee on Nationalised Industries (House of Commons paper 213, of 1959).

5. See H. A. Clegg, *Industrial Democracy and Nationalisation* (Blackwell, 1951).

6. Court of Enquiry (Cameron) on a dispute about railway pay. Cmd. 9352, of 1955, para. 10.

7. See M. Shanks (ed.), *Lessons of Public Enterprise* (Jonathan Cape, 1963), Ch. 4.

8. See *The Framework of Joint Consultation* (Acton Society Trust, 1952), and R. D. V. Roberts and H. Sallis, 'Joint Consultation in the Electricity Supply Industry 1949–59', in *Public Administration* (Summer 1959).

9. See Sir Arthur Street, *The Public Corporation in British Experience* (Allen & Unwin, 1947), Part III.

CHAPTER 5 : PROBLEMS OF ORGANISATION

1. This group consisted of the chairman of the London County Council; a representative of the official advisory committee on London traffic; the chairman of the Committee of London Clearing Bankers; the president of the Law Society; the president of the Institute of Chartered Accountants, and the chairman of the L.P.T.B. itself.

2. Clive Jenkins, *Power at the Top* (MacGibbon & Kee, 1959), p. 43.

3. Lord Simon of Wythenshawe, *The Boards of Nationalised Industries* (Longmans, 1957).

4. The Fleck and Herbert committees (discussed later in this chapter) have different views of this question. The Fleck report recommends career appointments until retiring age; the Herbert report suggests that 'security should be achieved by results rather than formal contract'.

5. *Public Enterprise*, p. 27.

6. Fleck report, p. 60, and Herbert report, p. 68.

7. See C. G. Lancaster, *The Organisation of the Coal Board* (1948), and *Structure and Control of the Coal Industry* (C.P.C., 1951).

8. N.C.B. report 1948, Appendix V.

9. *Report of the Advisory Committee on Organisation* (the Fleck report), N.C.B., 1955.

10. See Alan E. Thompson, 'Organisation in two nationalised industries,' *Scottish Journal of Political Economy* (June 1957).

11. There was, in fact, a report on the railways by a group headed by Sir Ivan Stedeford in 1960, but it was not published.

12. *Railways Reorganisation Scheme*. Cmnd. 9191, 1954.

13. Herbert report, p. 9.

CHAPTER 6 : CONTROL AND ACCOUNTABILITY

1. e.g. in the Coal Industry Nationalisation Act, 1946, section 3.

2. Select Committee on Nationalised Industries (House of Commons paper 120, 1955–6, para. 36).

3. See Select Committee on Nationalised Industries report (H. of C. paper 187–1, of 1958), pp. 50, 135.

4. *Hansard*, March 19th, 1956, col. 829 ff.

5. ibid., November 21st, 1961, col. 1145.

6. Cmnd. 1337, 1961.

7. Lords' *Hansard*, March 12th, 1953, col. 1504. This implies that the contact would be continuous and that the chairman would be a subordinate in an organisation run by the Minister.

8. Cmnd. 1248 (1960), pp. 7, 14.

9. Cmnd. 1337, p. 10, para. 30.

10. Attempts by the new Labour Government to restrain price increases in general led to renewed ministerial concern with public-enterprise prices in 1965. In some cases this took the form of reference to the National Board for Prices and Incomes, which is inevitably a clear and open procedure; and in any case there seemed to be a disposition to acknowledge that special restraint should lead to an adjustment of an industry's financial objective, openly declared.

11. The debate on the Address in reply to the Queen's Speech.

12. Lord Heyworth, evidence to the Select Committee on Nationalised Industries (H. of C. paper 235 of 1952–3), p. 84.

13. ibid.

14. S.C.N.I. Rep. 1957, p. 15.

15. Sir Toby Low, 'The Select Committee on Nationalised Industries', *Public Administration* (Spring 1962), p. 14.

16. The Comptroller and Auditor General is an independent officer of Parliament who audits Government accounts and calls the attention of the Public Accounts Committee to matters needing investigation.

17. H. of C. paper 276 (1959).

18. Sir Toby Low, op. cit., p. 9.

19. See G. L. McVey, 'The Public Accountability of Industry', *Political Quarterly* (October 1960).

20. A. H. Hanson, *Parliament and Public Ownership* (Cassell, 1961), p. 175.

21. ibid., p. 221.

CHAPTER 7 : AIMS OF NATIONALISATION

1. Coal Industry Nationalisation Act, 1946, section I (c).

2. See E. H. Phelps-Brown and J. Wiseman, *A Course in Applied Economics* (Pitman, 2nd ed., 1964).

3. I. M. D. Little, *The Price of Fuel* (O.U.P., 1953), p. 97.

4. Report on *National Policy for the Use of Fuel and Power Resources* (Cmnd. 8647, 1952), para. 66.

5. Herbert report (Cmd. 9672, p. 97), para. 372.

6. The Herbert report's 'Summary of Main Conclusions and Recommendations' contains all the points mentioned.

7. ibid., p. 139, para. 507.

8. A high rate of closures would mean, of course, labour disputes on a scale that would raise the actual costs of the N.C.B. very steeply, irrespective of the social consequences.

9. See, for example, *The assessment of priority for road improvements*, Road Research Laboratory Technical Paper 48 (H.M.S.O., 1960); C. D. Foster and M. E. Beesley, 'Estimating the Social Benefit of Constructing an Underground Railway in London', *Journal of the Royal Statistical Society* (1963) part I; and M. S. Feldstein, 'Cost-Benefit Analysis and Investment in the Public Sector', *Public Administration* (Winter 1964).

10. Not all change is for the better.

11. See Andrew Shonfield, *British Economic Policy since the War* (Penguin, 1958), and J. C. R. Dow, *The Management of the British Economy 1945–60* (C.U.P., 1964).

12. Report of the Select Committee on Nationalised Industries, 1957, p. 128, question 911, and 1958, p. xxiii, para. 124.

13. Cmnd. 1337 (April 1961).

14. ibid, para. 32. This solution implies, of course, that non-commercial activities are to be financed by cross-subsidisation.

15. ibid, para. 2.

16. ibid, para. 28.

17. John Hughes, *Nationalised Industries in the mixed economy* (Fabian Society, 1960), pp. 9–10.

18. e.g. the Coal Industry Nationalisation Act 1946, sec. I(a), states that the duties of the National Coal Board are 'working and getting the coal in Great Britain, to the exclusion (save as in this Act provided) of any other person'.

19. There may be strong buying monopolies (monopsonies) – e.g. the Central Electricity Generating Board's position as a purchaser of heavy generating equipment.

20. See essay by John Hughes in Shanks, *Lessons of Public Enterprise*, p. 143.

21. *Hansard*, March 31st, 1965, col. 1650.

22. Cmnd. 2651, paras. 20, 28.

23. In October 1964 the Minister of Transport (Mr Marples) ordered British Railways to raise their rates for carrying china clay, after protests by shipping interests, on the grounds that they were not charging the full cost of providing the service.

24. Report of the Committee on *National Policy for the use of Fuel and Power Resources* (Cmnd. 8647, 1952).

25. *Co-operation between Electricity and Gas Boards* (Cmnd. 695, 1959).

26. See Shanks, op. cit., ch. 8, p. 149, where this argument is set out at length by an anonymous young economist.

27. C. D. Foster, *The Transport Problem* (Blackie, 1963). In January 1966 Mr Foster was appointed Director General of Economic Planning at the Ministry of Transport.

CHAPTER 8 : POLITICS OF PUBLIC OWNERSHIP

1. Labour Party, *Let us win through together* (1950).

2. Labour Party, *The Future of Industrial Assurance* (1950). Some companies, such as the Liverpool Victoria, were already mutually owned.

3. Trades Union Congress, *Public Ownership: an interim report* (1953).

4. Labour Party, *Challenge to Britain* (1953).

5. There was no connection, of course, with earlier groups of 'revisionist' socialists, who were engaged in revising Marxist doctrine.

6. John Strachey, M.P., 'The Object of Further Socialisation', in the *Political Quarterly* (January 1953).

7. Hugh Gaitskell, *Socialism and Nationalisation* (Fabian Society, 1956), p. 18.

8. Speech by Jim Campbell, General Secretary of the National Union of Railwaymen, Labour Party *Annual Conference Report* (1957), p. 132.

9. Labour Party, *The New Britain* (September 1964), pp. 9, 10, 11, 14.

10. Hugh Gaitskell died in 1963.

11. The Conservative Party at least shared in the inception of the B.B.C., the Central Electricity Board, London Transport, B.O.A.C., the North of Scotland Hydro-Electric Board, and the Atomic Energy Authority.

12. Conservative and Unionist Central Office, 1949, p. 26.

13. Conservative and Unionist Party, *Manifesto* (September 1964), p. 12.

14. The Conservative Party spokesman on steel, Mr Iain Macleod, has declared that they would. *Hansard*, May 6th, 1965, col. 1598.

15. Liberal Publication Department, *The Liberal Manifesto: Think for Yourself* (1964), p. 5.

16. Reported in *The Times*, August 26th, 1964.

17. According to Richard Rose in Butler and King (*The British General Election of 1964* (Macmillan, 1965)), business firms and groups spent about £1,836,000 on political propaganda in the period before the election in October 1964.

18. Federation of British Industries, *Report on Nationalisation* (1958). It has also published its views on steel nationalisation in *British industry and the proposal to nationalise steel* (1965).

19. H. J. Laski, *Democracy in Crisis* (Allen & Unwin, 1933), contains perhaps the clearest statement of the thesis.

20. There are also 'profit-sharing' schemes, giving employees payments varying with profits (like dividends on shares), but no rights to a share in control.

21. A report to the Liberal Party by a committee under the chairmanship of Peter McGregor (June 1962).

22. Paul Derrick, *The Company and the Community*, and Norman Ross, *The Democratic Firm*, both Fabian Research pamphlets (1964). See also L. Tivey, 'The Reform of the Firm' in the *Political Quarterly* (April 1963).

Index

213